AS/A-LEVEL

Art & Design

Mark White

Philip Allan Updates
Market Place
Deddington
Oxfordshire
OX15 0SE

Tel: 01869 338652
Fax: 01869 337590
e-mail: sales@philipallan.co.uk
www.philipallan.co.uk

Printed by Raithby, Lawrence & Co Ltd, Leicester

P00108

Introduction

This dictionary is intended for AS and A2 art and design students. At any stage, in any unit of your course, it will help you to discover what specialist words mean, and to find out about art movements and specialist vocabulary in your work journals. Each entry contains one or more examples of works that you can follow up, and cross-references to other entries. You can use this dictionary to direct you to materials and how they work, or to follow through a particular theme. Most importantly, use the dictionary to lead you to the crucial formal elements that are the building blocks for making art, i.e. line, tone, colour, form, pattern and texture.

Each entry is made up of a series of parts, which vary according to the headword. All entries start with a basic definition of the word. Words in *italics* are cross-references that take you to other entries. Words in ***bold italic*** are of foreign origin.

When states the key period, time and context of the entry.

Who outlines the essential artists involved.

Links leads you to other relevant movements, artists and works. Where appropriate and possible, the link will give greater detail, which may guide you to creating work that you might wish to make as a result of reading the entry.

Formal elements tells you which of the vital building blocks of art are relevant to the entry and could be explored in your work.

How to use this dictionary

It is the start of a new unit, you have been given a theme, it is a bit bland and you do not know how to begin. This dictionary contains thematic words of the type you are likely to meet; it gives working definitions and, more importantly, directions, contextual studies, methods and materials to get your own art started.

A personal study, contextual studies guide

Looking at the work made by other artists and designers becomes increasingly important at AS and A-level. One of the difficulties you will encounter is that most of the relevant writing is by art historians who have a language all of their own. This dictionary should help you decode that language. After a few searches, you will be able to discuss the role of *impasto* within *Impressionist illusionism* with the best of them. Imagine that you have seen a work of art that looks interesting, part of an art movement you have never heard of, e.g. divisionism. Look it up and discover that *divisionism* was a French *Neo-Impressionist* style based around colour theory — general colour was broken down into contrasting colours put together in small dots to make their effect stronger. At the end of the entry there are links to, among other things, *colour* itself, which you know is one of the *formal elements* you have to cover in your coursework and exam. The links will also guide you to art works you can see, or find on the internet (there is a list of websites at the back of the dictionary). You keep following the dictionary links and become interested in *Minimalism*, an American art movement that appears to be the exact opposite to your starting point. Inspired by the Minimalist sculptor, Donald Judd, you make a series of perfect boxes.

A guide to methods and materials

What sort of paint should you use? You have been given some acrylic paint but are not sure what it is for. A full-page entry will tell you the different uses for acrylic, and lead on to the possible art studies, comparisons and techniques that could result from this medium.

A guide to ideas

The fundamental goal for all art is the exploration of ideas. Most of the entries in this dictionary discuss ideas and how artists have used them in the past, and continue to use them now. By following the links and their relationship to the formal elements you can become better informed, but more importantly, your own art work will become deeper, more interesting for you to create, and more interesting for others to look at.

Remember the central role of documentation in the AS/A2 exam, which requires that you show how you got to your final piece or outcome. Why, for instance, is the examiner looking at three white boxes, when the theme for your unit was colour and your art study was on divisionism? By using this dictionary, you can explain your thought processes as they develop, using specialist words to make others understand what you are trying to do.

A guide to location

This dictionary refers to hundreds of works of art and where they are to be found. Wherever possible, these works come from British museums and galleries, so that you can actually see them. Factors like scale, texture and colour are all very important and you can only really understand them by looking at the original work. However, displays change regularly, so please check before travelling a long way to see a particular piece of art. Many museum websites now detail which work is currently on display; a list of websites can be found at the back of the dictionary.

abstract: used to describe a work of art that does not try to look like an illusion of something else. This type of art is often called autonomous (meaning self-governing or independent), as it has no reference to anything outside the work. It can be actual, in the case of abstract painting, or notional, in the case of sculpture.

■ *When:* this normally applies to art from the twentieth century on, although the non-representational art of Muslim countries could also be termed abstract. It is difficult to be exact but the first truly abstract painting in the Western art tradition is thought to be 'Suprematist Square', 1914–15, Tretyakov, Moscow, by the Russian *Suprematist* artist Kasimir Malevich. Other artists were also working towards creating abstract art at the same time, for instance Wassily Kandinsky, who had produced a small painting known as 'First Abstract Watercolour', Musée National d'Art Moderne, Paris, signed 1910, but probably made some time later. These two works look very different, but they share similar characteristics in that they appear to be independent, referring to nothing but themselves. The shapes within the paintings are not drawn from nature, or *organic* forms, and certainly in the case of Suprematism and the later art movement *De Stijl*, the references were to standard geometric shapes.

At first, abstract art, like that of De Stijl, for example, was part of the search for Utopia that characterises most art of the early twentieth century. After the Second World War, critics saw abstract art as deliberately different from the *Socialist Realist* art of the USSR and the earlier *Nazi* and fascist art of Germany and Italy. Socialist Realism showed illusionistic images of the glorious struggle of the workers of the communist state — abstract must be better, because it was made by the capitalist West. It is important to realise that although art might be created alone in a studio, it is usually received by a society that will interpret art objects according to political, rather than artistic, or *aesthetic*, rules.

■ *Who:* abstract painting tends to divide into two halves: geometric and a looser, more *expressionist* style. Geometric painting was represented first by Suprematism and then by the new 'universal language' of abstract art, De Stijl, e.g. Mondrian's 'Composition', 1929, Solomon R. Guggenheim Museum, New York. This led eventually to *Op art* and *Minimalism*, e.g. Sol LeWitt's 'Fifteen part drawing using four colours and all variations', 1970, Tate Modern, London. A more personal style, developed by *Post-Impressionist* artists like van Gogh, who used the *autographic mark,* led to the freeing of *colour* from its purely descriptive role that became so important for *Expressionism* (from 1905 until about 1930). This culminated in the fully abstract art of the *Abstract Expressionists,* who conveyed strong emotions through their use of paint.

In sculpture the work of the Russian *Constructivist,* Vladimir Tatlin, between 1913 and 1916 represented some of the first three-dimensional abstract works, e.g. 'Project for a Monument for the Third International' 1919 — the plan for a huge double spiral spanning the River Neva in Moscow, a vast symbol of revolution. Anthony Caro, the British sculptor, was much influenced by Abstract Expressionism and is usually thought to be the first entirely abstract sculptor, e.g. 'Early One Morning', 1962, Tate Britain, London.

■ *Links:* Abstract Expressionism, art object, autographic mark, colour, Constructivism, De Stijl, Minimalism, Op art, Post-Impressionism, Suprematism.

■ *Formal elements:* in purely abstract art all the *formal elements* are particularly significant — they are the major reason for the genesis of the work. In certain periods some elements are more important, e.g. pattern in De Stijl, and texture in Abstract Expressionism.

Abstract Expressionism: the name for the many types of large, mostly *gestural painting,* based initially in the United States, in which artists no longer made narratives referring to the world outside the picture or used traditional methods. The key American Abstract Expressionist, Jackson Pollock, for instance, poured or dripped his paint onto an unprimed *canvas* stretched out on the floor. In 'One (number 31, 1959)' from 1950, Museum of Modern Art, New York, a huge painting, 270 cm by 531 cm, the trails of black, white and green household enamel paint record the rhythmic movements of the artist's arm. The critic Harold Rosenberg said in 1952, 'The canvas began to appear to one American painter after another as an arena in which to act'. Since late *Impressionism* and *Cubism*, artists had increasingly made the process of creating art the subject of their work, and there are strong visual parallels between Pollock's work and Monet's last paintings of water lilies and wisteria at Giverny from about 1918–23.

There was no specific Abstract Expressionist style or movement; Willem de Kooning's paintings, for example, were almost representational. His 'Women' series from the 1950s, e.g. 'The Visit', 1966–67, Tate Modern, London, are recognisable, if violent, distortions of the female form. Pollock's use of *automatism* was not shared by Mark Rothko, whose large flat areas of intense sombre colour, e.g. 'Black on Maroon', 1958–59, Tate Modern, London (see *Colour Field*

Painting), have more to do with a spiritual search. These three important artists, in common with other Abstract Expressionists, shared an intense belief in self-expression; the need for the creation of art to investigate their own psychology and the collective unconscious. Like earlier *abstract* artists, they believed that associations with the outside world must be removed from art for it to have any truth or relevance to universal human existence.

Abstract art had a particular role after the Second World War (see *abstract*). Although many of the main painters were European, Abstract Expressionism was the first major development in American art to achieve international fame. As a result of its influence and importance, New York, rather than Paris, became the centre of the art scene in the mid-twentieth century. Note that Pollock's paintings were not made with a brush onto a canvas standing on an *easel* in the traditional European manner, but were vigorously and athletically made on the floor.

■ *When:* started in the 1940s, reaching its characteristic form by the 1950s, it became the leading type of international art in the 1950s and 1960s.

■ *Who:* Jackson Pollock, Willem de Kooning, Barnett Newman, Mark Rothko; key critics were Clement Greenberg and Harold Rosenberg.

■ *Links: abstract, Action Painting, automatism, Expressionism, gestural painting, Modernism, Surrealism.*

■ *Formal elements:* colour in Rothko, texture in de Kooning, Pollock.

abstraction: describes the process whereby the artist moves away from representing the world to making art that is purely *abstract* with no obviously natural content.

■ *When:* abstraction is a twentieth-century phenomenon. *Cubist* abstraction never quite became purely abstract; Cubist paintings always contained just enough references to the real world to make the viewer perceive that the painting was about something. However, Cubism was the spur for most artists' approach to abstraction.

■ *Who:* all art is in some ways a process of abstraction from nature, but the classic example of the process is Mondrian's series of paintings of apple trees, the sea and church towers from 1910 to 1914, which led to his pure *Neo-Plastic* abstract works.

■ *Links: Cubism, De Stijl.*

■ *Formal elements:* all.

acrylic: a type of synthetic or polymer paint that has various important properties for the student:

● Acrylic paint is relatively cheap and easy to buy and comes in various grades, 'artist' being the most expensive and longest lasting, with the strongest pigments. The cheapest grades are often called 'student', and whilst the quality

a

of pigment, especially yellow, is not as good, they are usually sufficient. It is possible to buy bulk acrylic mediums and the pigments to mix into them, but unless you are intending to use vast quantities, they are not necessary.

- Acrylic paint is water-soluble but water-resistant once dry; this means it can be thinned easily to behave like a *watercolour wash* and can create *impasto* either straight from the tube or with the addition of other media, e.g. sand, to give it extra bulk. Adding a very small amount of washing-up liquid helps the paint flow better.

- The colours of acrylic paints are strong and are inclined to look artificial if not mixed carefully. However, they can produce exciting, lively-looking work. The paint surface is characteristically flat, but the slight shine given by the polymer nature of the paint reflects light well; this can be increased by adding PVA-type glue, or decreased by adding matt medium.

- Acrylic paint dries quickly, so it is suitable for use within restricted lesson time. If you cover a palette with cling-film to keep the air out, it will last for a day or so before drying out completely. You can buy retarders to slow drying times — useful if, for instance, you are trying to blend large areas of colour. Do not use too much, as this will produce a film on the surface which makes wrinkles and takes days to dry properly.

- Acrylic is flexible so it can be painted on any surface — paper, canvas or board. These can be primed if you wish, but acrylic paint will take easily to most unprimed surfaces without laborious preparation.

■ *Links: Abstract Expressionism, additive mixing, Pop art, subtractive mixing.* See Hockney's 'A Bigger Splash', 1967, Tate Liverpool. A painting of a pool in Los Angeles, the canvas is divided by broad flat areas of colour with sharp edges (straight edges created by masking tape is another characteristic of this medium). The 'Splash', though painted in acrylic, is a parody of the *gestural painting* in oils made by the preceding art movement *Abstract Expressionism*. It might be worth comparing the results of the two media as a personal, contextual study, or as a work journal art study before making your own art.

■ *When:* acrylic paint became widely available from the 1960s.

■ *Who:* it was much used by the *Pop artists*. David Hockney's large flat canvases owe a great deal to the characteristics of acrylic.

■ *Formal elements:* colour, tone, texture.

Action Painting: a way of painting with huge, visible brushwork in which, without first drawing (see ***alla prima***), the paint is spontaneously brushed, dripped or thrown on to the canvas and where the psychological intention of the artist is the key to the action. For this to work, the painting has to move away from the *easel*, usually to be stretched on the floor. The final work is a record of the movements of the artist and the process of making rather than a planned *composition*.

■ *When:* the American art critic, Harold Rosenberg, first used the term Action Painting in 1952 — 'what was to go on canvas was not a picture but an event'. Action Painting is generally used to describe the characteristically *gestural painting* of *Abstract Expressionism* from the late 1940s to early 1950s in the United States, although the notion of the spontaneous movements of the artist had its roots in the earlier European *Surrealist* concept of *automatism*.

■ *Who:* Jackson Pollock in particular, but also de Kooning. These spontaneous methods had a following in postwar Europe, France in particular, e.g. Tachism's painted marks that had not been obviously worked on by the conscious or cultivated mind.

■ *Links:* Abstract Expressionism, automatism, Post-Impressionism.

■ *Formal elements:* pattern and texture.

additive mixing: a method of colour mixing, so called because light rays are added rather than blended. Isaac Newton showed that when white light (daylight) passes through a prism it breaks down into the full colour spectrum. In other words, white light contains all the colours of the rainbow: red, orange, yellow, yellow-green, blue-green, blue, violet and, important for additive mixing, when you recombine all the rays, the colour returns to white. The usual system of colour pigment mixing with normal opaque paint, called full body colour, is the method that most of us are familiar with: yellow plus blue equals green, etc. Additive mixing with light is not the same as mixing pigments; in the additive system a magenta, a cyan blue and a medium yellow are the three primaries. Additive mixing is mostly used in printing, colour photography and lighting. However, remembering that in light all the primaries added together make white, this method has two basic applications in painting.

● You can mimic the process of additive mixing by using layers of transparent glazes on white paper. Mix and apply very thin layers of *acrylic* paint, waiting for each layer to dry before applying the next, making sure that you can always see through to the paper. Transparent glazes used in this fashion can behave slightly like additive colours, in that each layer of the glaze can be seen at the same time, and they reflect less white light than opaque paint. If you can see all the colours at once, then you are starting to recombine the colours of the spectrum and the result will be much brighter than if you had used the usual *subtractive mixing* system. The other method, best suited to working on a large scale, is to mix water-based, strongly coloured inks with a PVA-type glue and then scrape thin layers onto the paper. Again, each layer must be dry before you put on the next one. The combined colours should be lighter and more stimulating to the eye than if the mixture had been made on the palette.

● *Divisionist* artists used the additive process by painting small points of pure primaries to create additive mixtures when viewed from a distance. This technique can also be hinted at by mixing your colours on the canvas, paper or board, but not doing it too well so that additive mixing will result from bad blending.

■ *Links:* aerial perspective, Colour Field Painting, divisionism, hue, saturation, subtractive mixing.

■ *Formal elements:* colour.

aerial perspective: refers to a technique used to create depth and space on a two-dimensional surface through the different spatial effects of cold colours, i.e. blue appears to move away from the viewer and is used in the *background* of a painting. Remember that the sky is not really blue — it only appears so because blue light (short wavelengths) is scattered by dust or haze in the atmosphere more strongly than red light (longer wavelengths). Hills in the distance appear blue because blue light penetrates haze more easily.

■ *Who:* a technique used by the Romans, e.g. the House of the Vettii, Pompeii, first century AD, and revived by Leonardo da Vinci, e.g. the landscape in the 'Virgin and Child with St Anne', 1508–10, Musée du Louvre, Paris. Used to great effect by many landscape artists since, e.g. Claude's 'Marriage of Isaac and Rebekah', 1648, National Gallery, London; J. M. W. Turner, for instance in the background of 'The Fighting Temeraire', 1838, National Gallery, London, where the blue of the distant river banks is contrasted with the astonishing red and gold of the rising sun.

■ *Links: illusionism.* Other techniques, used first by Leonardo da Vinci, include *sfumato*, or smokiness, to create the effect of haze and the loss of distinct contrasts on the distant horizon. This system was used throughout the history of landscape painting from Leonardo to *Impressionism*, but firmly rejected by the *Fauves*. These are all methods to experiment with, and need not be restricted to huge landscape subjects; the properties of warm and cold colours can also be used in small-scale, still life works.

■ *Formal elements:* colour, tone.

aesthetics: a branch of philosophy concerned with the study of such concepts as beauty and taste. It is important for art because it deals with the feelings, concepts and judgements we have about beauty and about art itself. If a work is described as 'aesthetically pleasing', then it has met most of the criteria on somebody's list of beautiful things, but what is on that list? How did it get there? What is a work of art anyway?

African art: a category which strictly speaking does not exist, because the separation between objects and their use that characterises Western art does not apply. A uniform style of art made across this huge continent has never existed. Since the *Renaissance* the European concept of art has made a divide between the use of an object and what it looks like — the difference between *fine art* and *craft*. The objects that we now categorise as African art were both functional and beautiful. For instance, a pair of entrance doors made by Olowe of Ise in Ikere (Nigeria) in 1916, now in the British Museum, contain a series of powerful high relief carvings, one of which shows the visit of the local white administrator. These were working doors, art objects and social commentary all at once.

There are two areas to look at under this heading: art from Africa itself and the use made by European artists of African art, usually objects which early twentieth-century artists discovered in European museums.

Art from Africa obviously varies according to the part of this huge country it comes from (an area of about 12 million square miles) and the time it was made. Bear in mind that people have been living and making art here since the human species began; the earliest African objects date from about 1.6 million years ago. Within that time frame the influence of Europeans was relatively late, and an unhappy one for many Africans. Most of the well-known African sculptures were made by those who had settled and started farming. Art of any scale demands some sort of stability so that work can be preserved and techniques and ideas developed, and, of course, the time in which to make it. Wood was the major medium used and, logically enough, the major areas of wood sculpture in Africa are those that have the best supplies of timber, although bronze and, particularly, iron were also important, as were textiles, pottery and rock paintings.

African work with wood south of the Sahara rarely employed carpentry; it depended on carving, usually from a single piece of wood. This affects the shape and scale of the sculpture and tends to be the main unifying feature of this form of African art. Such a restriction also allows the carver to show the shape of the original tree in the final work, using the rising grain of the wood to describe a figure for example, and this restriction is the major visual connection between most African wooden sculptures. The characteristic marks of the carving tools are another connection; sharp incisions or cuts, often in regular patterns, a technique that can also be seen carried over into much of the pottery.

In Europe, African art was seen in Paris from the 1890s, not only in the museums, but also in local shops, brought back by people travelling to the French African colonies. The art that is familiar to us, as well as to those early twentieth-century Parisian artists, came from central Africa — mostly fetishes (objects which control or express natural or supernatural forces or beings) and masquerades (dances and festivals for which a wide variety of masks survive). These formed part of what could often be a huge costume covering the whole human performer, e.g. 'Ceremonial Mask' from Wobe, Ivory Coast, late 1800s, Musée de l'Homme, Paris.

The most well-known European use of African art first appeared in 'Les

Demoiselles d'Avignon', 1907, Museum of Modern Art, New York, painted by Picasso in Paris — his crucial pre-*Cubist* painting. However, the idea of painting naked woman in poses which look deliberately separate from the traditions of European art, and which include specific references to art from non-European sources, came first from Gauguin, e.g. 'The Spectre Watches Over Her' ('man'o tupapa'u'), 1892, Albright Knox Art Gallery, Buffalo, New York, which shows a naked Tahitian girl lying on a bed, with textiles beneath her and strange shapes and figures behind. The first sculptural use of African forms, i.e. short legs, thick thighs, a long body and either a very large or a very small head, is usually assumed to be by the *Fauvist* painter, Andre Derain, e.g. his 'Crouching Figure' of 1907, Réunion des Musée Nationaux, Paris — a small, sturdy, stone figure with large, solid feet and simplified hands, important for its use of direct and obvious carving in stone. The sculptor Brancusi, who started working in early twentieth-century Paris, was influenced by characteristics of African wooden sculpture. His reduction of three-dimensional form to its basic shapes owes a great deal to African work, e.g. 'The First Step', 1913, Musée National d'Art Moderne, Centre Georges Pompidou, Paris.

If you look at the figures in Picasso's 'Les Demoiselles d'Avigon' and the style in which they are painted, each one comes from a radically different source. The face of the left-hand figure seems to be a combination of Egyptian profile with Gauginesque heavy line drawing. The central women's faces are based on Iberian sculpture in the Louvre, and the two on the right from African carvings that Picasso collected. This type of work, its simplification and use of powerful line, was something that Matisse had probably first investigated by looking at sculptures from the Congo; it was these that he subsequently showed to Picasso.

The German *Expressionist* Kirchner also took inspiration from the African sculptures and carvings by the Palau Islanders he found in the Ethnographisches Museum in Dresden, telling his friends about them in the same way that Matisse told Picasso about Congolese art. Later Expressionist art owed a great debt to these earlier discoveries, particularly in the powerful, aggressive use of jagged line in the *woodcuts*, e.g. the title woodcut of 'Chronik der Kunstler-gruppe Brücke', 1913, Wallraf-Richartz Museum, Cologne.

Why was this non-European art so relevant to these early *Modernist* artists? During the later nineteenth century the European powers had been exploiting Africa and dividing the land up into colonies, particularly in the Congo; slavery was only finally outlawed in 1863. Africa represented not only Europe's opposite, enticing to the *avant-garde* looking for something other than academic naturalistic tricks or empty *Impressionist* pastiches of the *Salon*, but in the post-Darwinian age (*Origin of Species*, 1859, and the *Descent of Man*, 1871) Africa, known as the 'dark continent', was also seen as the country of Europe's childhood, a place without scientific rationalism and the application of reason, still subject to uncontrolled sexuality. Sigmund Freud, who had published his *Interpretation of Dreams* in 1896, and the *Psychopathology of Everyday Life* in 1904, used this opposite nature as a familiar analogy when he called women the 'dark continent'. Freud's fundamental importance as the father of psychoanalysis was in pointing out the influence of the unconscious over conscious behaviour and the sexual origin of neuroses, later to become essential for *Surrealism*. In other words, for late nineteenth- and early twentieth-century artists, African art was important, not just for the excitement of the new shapes and ways of representing the figure, but also because it represented something disturbing and completely apart from the accepted European way of behaving: the Other.

It is here that we need to acknowledge the inappropriate use of the word 'primitive'. Much of the African art plundered by the colonial powers and displayed in European museums was until relatively recently labelled primitive. This term depended on a series of false assumptions, mostly on the frankly racist notion that the societies and people that produced this work were in many ways lower down the evolutionary scale (re Darwin) and therefore less sophisticated. For artists, this meant that Africans were closer to the true emotions of humanity, but for others it meant that they were farther away from 'civilisation'.

The interest in African art showed by the Cubists, Expressionists and *Post-Impressionists*, among others, led to new treatments of the human form — the characteristic angular, almost detached, planes of Cubism and Expressionism for example. This in turn led to the new use of space in art, the rejection of the conventional perspective that had characterised art since the Renaissance.

More recently, artists have used African art as a way of exploring their own identity. Marcus Garvey's African-American debates in the 1960s sparked considerable interest among Afro-Caribbeans, spawning both Rastafarian music and art forms that used African textiles as a way of symbolising a return to a people's original roots. The multi-layered, referential approach of *Postmodernism* has allowed many, mostly American, artists to explore similar themes, e.g. Jean Michel Basquiat. Originally a graffiti artist in New York who was taken up by Andy Warhol, his work is a combination of previous fine art forms, street art and African themes, e.g. 'Boy and Dog in a Johnnypump', 1982, Galerié Bruno Bishofberger, Zurich, which shows a dread-locked man painted in a vivid sketch-like manner using black and red against splashy yellow, green and pink brushstrokes — a combination of painterliness and comic art. The art historian Robert Farris has called this style 'Afro-Atlantic vividness'. Or there is the artist working in Britain, Yinka Shonibare, e.g. 'How does a girl like you, get to be a girl like you?', 1995, Saatchi Collection, London. This displays draped mannequins in Victorian-style dresses, but made from contemporary African cloth, making reference to Victorian colonialism and the role of shopping in today's culture. Chris Ofili is another artist exploring similar themes, using swirling patterns, resin and elephant dung in his paintings, which feature figures with obvious African and Black American motifs, e.g. 'Afrodizzia', 1996, Saatchi Collection, London.

■ *Links: Cubism, Expressionism, woodcut.* Think of the role of the environment in art: artwork made in the desert, e.g. the Tuareg portable beds of the Sahara, will be very different from, for instance, the wooden statues of the Zulus of Southern Africa. The properties of the different materials available will produce very different work. How, for example, do the textiles vary from one area of the country to another? Who does the weaving in different societies? In some of the societies south of the Sahara, men and women might both weave cloth, but they will use separate looms; will those differences affect the end product? Much of the art from this continent uses the human figure — how has proportion been arranged? How does that arrangement compare to the European view of the figure, and can you combine the two in your own work? Hairstyles are an important identifying feature for many cultures; some of these have been preserved through masks and figure sculptures. They could be a very fertile area for investigation — after all, hair is still an issue today. In more recent work, personal or cultural identity is a crucial theme and is represented by objects that have social or ritual significance, often presented as a form of installation that combines traditional craft techniques, e.g. weaving, with contemporary methods like reusing tin cans to make bags and boxes. These are all processes and ideas that could be very fruitful in an art room.

■ *Formal elements:* all, but form was the most significant for the early twentieth-century artists.

afterimage: when you look at two contrasting colours side by side, or stare at a single colour for any length of time, the receptors in the retina appear to produce another colour, the *complementary* of the original *hue*.

■ *Links: colour, divisionism, Op art.*

alla prima: an Italian term, first used in the *Renaissance* to describe a method of painting in which the picture is painted without a sketch (or underpainting) setting out the *composition*, and carried out in a single layer of paint.

■ *Who: Impressionism* was probably the high point of *figurative* **alla prima** painting, more controlled than *Abstract Expressionism*, which probably marked its non-figurative high point.

■ *Links: Abstract Impressionism, Impressionism, Renaissance.*

allegory: literally means 'saying something else'. Allegory refers to art that uses one subject to symbolise another, usually moral concepts such as good and evil. The use of allegory dates back to the *Classical*, e.g. 'The Winged Victory of Samothrace', 190 BC, Musée du Louvre, Paris, a marble sculpture showing Nike, the winged goddess of victory, commemorating a naval battle — the concept of victory made into a visible person or god.

■ *When:* allegory was the usual medium through which Western art conveyed its message until *Modernism* began to take away the literary content.

■ *Links:* figurative, Pre-Raphaelites, Romanticism, Symbolism. Post-Second World War German artists have used allegory as a way of exploring the effect of their country's Nazi past, e.g. Anselm Keifer's 'Parsifal III', 1973, Tate Modern, London, which, like most of his art, explores past German myths. Parsifal was a legendary medieval figure about whom Wagner (who was much loved by the Nazis) wrote an opera (first performed in 1882) exploring the conflict between Christianity and paganism, good and evil, darkness and light, using allegory.

Postmodernism marked the return to *figurative* multi-layered art, and allegory has again become a standard part of the repertoire. For instance, Cindy Sherman's representation of herself as a series of different stereotypical female film stars, e.g. 'Untitled Film Still No. 17', 1977, Tate Modern, London, shows her in a posed image, part of an unknown imaginary narrative, a situation that asks questions about the role of the media.

all-over painting: a painting style whereby the canvas is covered with an unfocused structure of paint and form without obvious *composition*.

■ *Who:* the term is usually applied to Jackson Pollock's *Action Paintings*, although it could also apply to late Monet, as much as to *gestural painting*, or *Abstract Expressionism*.

■ *Links: Abstract Expressionism, Action Painting, composition, Impressionism.*

■ *Formal elements:* pattern, texture.

Analytical Cubism: see *Cubism.*

anamorphosis: an extreme form of perspective, this is a method of distorting a two-dimensional image so that it can only be recognised when the viewer stands in a particular place or looks through a special device.

■ *Who:* Hans Holbein, 'The Ambassadors', 1533, National Gallery, London. A *portrait* of two men with many of their possessions on display, but at the bottom of the painting is a strange shape. If you stand about 2 metres to the right of the painting you can make out the image of a skull, a ***memento mori***, or symbol of death, reminding the young men in the painting that despite their obvious wealth, death comes to us all and that the spiritual life is equally important.

■ *Links: perspective, **Vanitas**.*

■ *Formal elements:* form, shape.

annotation: the method of making notes on and around a reproduction of the work of art being studied; it is a key skill in AS/A-level art. In your *work journal* you could reproduce an image by using one of the following methods: making a clear sketch of the work, making a photocopy, sticking in a postcard or

a

downloading the image from the website where you found it. Place relevant information around that image, pointing out areas of importance with arrows. Dorling Kindersley's *Annotated Guide to Art* (see the bibliography at the end of the dictionary) is a useful model.

If you choose to make a sketch, it need not involve the whole painting, as long as the basic *formal elements* are covered, neither should it take longer than a couple of short lessons to complete. The sketch is not an end in itself. The point of this exercise is not to create a perfect copy; making another version of the painting is pointless. The role of annotation is to show what you have learnt, how this art relates to the art of its own time (*contemporary*) and art since, and more importantly, how that learning is relevant to the *theme* you are studying. Merely copying chunks of biography and other people's opinions only shows that you are good at copying. You must be able to show an examiner that you are looking for a purpose. Always ask yourself the basic question: what is the relevance of this work to my own art?

antique, the: a term for Greek and Roman antiquity.
■ *When:* begins *c.* 2000 BC, ends *c.* 500 AD. The antique was particularly important as a source of inspiration for the artists of the *Renaissance* and *Neo-classicism*.
■ *Links: Classical/classicism, Renaissance.*

aquatint: a print from a copper plate produced by the same technique as *etching*. A finished aquatint has a similar grainy quality and tonality to a *watercolour* painting, because the areas between the etched lines are covered with a powdered resin that protects the surface from the biting process of the acid bath.

Goya, the Spanish painter and printmaker and the most powerful European artist of his day, developed the process of aquatint in his astonishing series of 'Los Caprichos' ('The Caprices'), 1793–98. These were 82 plates that integrated both etching and aquatint in the same process, rather than etching first and then superimposing the aquatint to impose a tonal ground afterwards, as had happened before. If you look, for instance, at 'Soplones' ('Blowers'), number 48 of Goya's 'Los Caprichos', 1799, Victoria and Albert Museum, London, it is a very strong image full of frightening creatures who are creating terror in a man by blowing into his ear. The varying depth of etched line is set against soft areas of aquatint ground — a technological advance used to create a terrifying representation.

armature: the framework, skeleton or internal structure used in *sculpture* to support the modelling material, e.g. chicken wire and plaster, papier maché or clay.

■ *Links: sculpture.*

art: a creative activity which produces works of beauty or other special significance. Artists and critics since Marcel Duchamp (French-born experimental artist and art theorist) have been interpreting the term in different ways, so that the word 'art' is harder to define than ever. A simple working definition would be: an actual or implied object or activity that demands the use of your senses, in particular thought. Remember that all art is a form of communication and expression, made to be exhibited in some way or other.

The AS/A-level in art offers students either the broad-based unendorsed course (art and design) or a more specialised *endorsed* programme, which includes the following: art and design, fine art, three-dimensional design, textiles, photography, graphic design, and critical and contextual studies in art.

Art Brut: a term invented by the French artist Jean Dubuffet for art produced by mental patients, prisoners, etc. — people outside the established art world, who are untrained in art. The English term is Outsider art. Dubuffet was strongly influenced by the wartime graffiti of occupied Paris; his pictures feature thick pastes incorporating earth and sand in the paint, which he scratched with sticks. He also created sculptures out of junk materials. Art Brut was spontaneous, unprocessed and consciously different from the traditional Western stereotypes of what art should look like — after all, that culture had just produced the Holocaust and the atom bomb.

■ *When:* from the late 1940s.

■ *Who:* the key artist was Jean Dubuffet who introduced Art Brut into his own work, e.g. 'Monsieur Plume with creases in his trousers (portrait of Henri Michaux)', 1947, Tate Modern, London.

■ *Links: Abstract Expressionism, Pop art.* David Hockney, like many artists in the late 1950s, used Dubuffet's techniques of scratching and roughening the surface, using graffiti and childlike art to express his 'otherness', e.g. 'We Two Boys Together Clinging', 1961, Arts Council of Great Britain.

■ *Formal elements:* texture, pattern.

Arte Povera: an Italian art movement characterised by the use of natural materials such as earth, sticks, water and newspaper; works that depended upon an acute awareness of the different qualities of the cheap materials used. Many *Arte Povera* works featured contrasting substances or objects, e.g. Luciano Fabro's 'Ovaries' of 1988, Tate Modern, London, which shows steel cables containing polished marble egg shapes; the dark colour and strength of the metal contrast with the white, easily fractured marble. The intention of *Arte Povera* artists was to make sculptural work that questioned the status of art itself by using pre-existing objects, e.g. Mario Merz's 'Do we turn round inside houses, or is it houses which turn around us?', 1977, Tate Modern, London. This round, house-like structure is made from metal, stone and glass, but also uses electric light. It combines references to ancient crafts like basket weaving with fundamental questions about the nature of shelter and a political attack on the commercialisation of modern society and the art gallery system. Richard Long, the British *Land artist*, had strong links with **Arte Povera**, and both movements were connected with *Conceptual art*. **Arte Povera**'s status as an influential Italian development meant it was able to assess the legacy of Italian art and society for *contemporary* art movements. When looking at Fabro's sculpture 'Ovaries', remember that Italy is a Catholic country that forbids the use of contraception.

■ *Who:* Luciano Fabro, Jannis Kounellis, Michelangelo Pistoletto, Mario Merz.
■ *When:* 1962–72.
■ *Links:* art object, Conceptual art, found object, Land art.
■ *Formal elements:* texture, form.

Art Nouveau: a decorative style in art, craft and design originating in Belgium and France, which quickly spread across Europe and the United States. It was also very influential in architecture. The Art Nouveau style was based on plant forms and is characterised by what is called 'the whiplash line' — an asymmetrical curving line that varies in thickness as it continuously doubles back on itself, creating a great sense of movement and liveliness.

The popularity of Art Nouveau resulted in a growing closeness between high or *fine art* (painting and sculpture) and arts and *crafts* (applied art). A good example of this style in architecture can be seen in Charles Rennie Mackintosh's School of Art in Glasgow, 1908, where the ironwork on the windows is not only very decorative — the thin strips of iron pulled into twisting knots — but it has the practical purpose of forming brackets for window cleaners' ladders. The ironwork also supports the large, plain, grid-like windows. For many people, the first introduction to Art Nouveau are the entrances to the metro stations in Paris. Designed by Hector Guimard in 1900, the entrance to the Bastille station, for example, is an *organic* growth of wrought iron and coloured glass, built around the curving, characteristic Art Nouveau line. The emphasis on this sort of stylised pattern-making in design contributed to the development of abstract art. Look at early Mondrian, e.g. 'The Grey Tree', 1912, Gemeentemuseum, The Hague, where you can see the characteristic whiplash line. The sinuous curve is apparent in much of Edvard Munch's work, which had a profound influence on *Expressionism*. See in particular 'The Scream', 1893, National Gallery, Oslo.

■ *When:* 1880s–1914.
■ *Who:* Aubrey Beardsley, Antoni Gaudi, Hector Guimard, Gustav Klimt, Charles Rennie Mackintosh, Louis Comfort Tiffany.
■ *Links:* De Stijl, organic, Post-Impressionism.
■ *Formal elements:* colour, line.

art object: even by late *Impressionism* it was clear that artists were beginning to consider the *canvas* as an object in itself, rather than a view into an illusory world (see *perspective*). The logical process of *abstraction* is that the art work will be seen as complete in itself; this, coupled with greater awareness of art as a commodity that existed in a financial as well as *aesthetic* space, led to the term the 'art object' as a broad description of what artists make. *Conceptual* artists in the 1960s concerned themselves largely with ideas, and felt their work was leading to the dematerialisation or disappearance of the art object. Artists earn their money by selling what they create (see *art*), so art objects will always exist in some form.

Arts and Crafts movement: an English movement that combined *fine art* with *crafts* and architecture to increase the importance of handicraft as factory production took over. It was inspired by the 1851 Great Exhibition at the Crystal Palace in London, in reaction to the inferior machine-made design that was displayed there, and as an attempt to revive domestic architecture (local styles that belong to the area in which they are built). Arts and Crafts adherents felt that the only important work was that made by hand, with enjoyment. William Morris (see below) called art 'the expression by man of pleasure in his labour'.
- **When:** late nineteenth century.
- **Who:** William Morris is probably the best known of the Arts and Crafts writers and designers, mostly through his interior designs. His medieval-inspired, nature-based patterns in wallpaper and textiles are still popular today and often used in school projects to demonstrate repeat pattern. Writers like Morris made the key connection between the conditions in which art is made and the subsequent quality of that art. Augustus Pugin was the *Gothic* Revival architect and designer responsible for the Gothic-inspired designs and ornaments used on the Houses of Parliament, 1836–65. John Ruskin was the influential writer and critic on architecture and art, who championed the English landscape painter J. M. W. Turner.
- **Links:** *Art Nouveau*, which was dependent on the Arts and Crafts movement for its nature-based, irregular curves and whiplash-like line.

The Arts and Crafts movement was responsible for an approach to building that led to architects believing it was important to show how a structure was made and that what happened on the inside should be reflected in the structure of the outside — see, for instance, Morris' Red House, Philip Webb, 1859, Bexley Heath, Kent, where the windows have been put where they are needed, rather than where the architectural style dictates. The design of the Red House marks the beginning of a design movement that led to the most radical architecture of the twentieth century, e.g. the Lloyds Building, Richard Rogers, 1978–86. In this building all the facilities (lifts, lavatories, kitchens, fire escape stairways, etc.) are attached to the side of the basic structure, and can be removed or changed if the use of the building changes. There is little obvious connection between the two buildings, but the underlying stress on function in the Lloyds Building can be traced back to the Arts and Crafts Movement.

The Arts and Crafts belief in handicraft, and the removal of the fine art/craft divide, led directly to the initial ideas behind the *Bauhaus*, the most important art school in the first half of the twentieth century, and therefore to the development of abstract art in the second half of the twentieth century.

The *Pre-Raphaelite Brotherhood*, whose first phase was from 1848 to about 1853, was profoundly influenced by William Morris and John Ruskin — Morris collaborated with members of the group on occasion. The Brotherhood produced intensely detailed paintings based on a very close study of nature and a technique of working paint into a wet white ground to intensify already bright colours, e.g. Millais' 'Christ in the House of his Parents', 1850, London.
■ *Formal elements:* line, form, tone, pattern.

assemblage: term describing the technique of making three-dimensional *collages* using natural or man-made materials such as cardboard, sheet metal, wood and household rubbish. These were formed into sculptures by being glued, welded, combined or constructed (adding one bit to another). Why is this method important? Assemblage represented a rejection of the traditional methods of making sculpture — carving, which takes away materials, or modelling, which builds up material into a shape which is then usually cast (see *sculpture*).
■ *Who:* the key work is Pablo Picasso's 'Guitar' from 1912, Museum of Modern Art, New York, an open and flimsy construction of planes, made from man-made materials in the same process as *Cubist* collage. Like collage, assemblage asserts the tangibility of the sculpture; it represents something and is an object in its own right. It not only captures the three-dimensionality of the world revealed to the eye, but it also draws attention to itself as a three-dimensional form (see *art object*). Like Cubist paintings, space in Picasso's sculpture and subsequent assemblage is given solidity and became another formal element for sculptures.
■ *Links: collage, Cubism, combine painting, Dada, Junk art, ready-made, sculpture, Surrealism.* The other important usage of assemblage after Picasso (see *Cubism*) was the emphasis on non-art materials, specifically rubbish, e.g. Kurt Schwitters, *Merz* collages, or Rauschenberg's combine paintings, e.g. 'Canyon', 1959, Private Collection, New York, that features a stuffed eagle, photographs, paint tubes and a pillow (see *collage*). See also how ordinary objects have been used in an art context, e.g. *Dada*, Duchamp's *ready-mades* and the *Surrealist* artist Meret Oppenheim's fur cup and saucer, 'Luncheon in Fur', 1936, Museum of Modern Art, New York.
■ *Formal elements:* form.

autographic mark: term describing the identifiable and personal style of an artist. In the same way that we each have handwriting whose form and style is personal to us, and from which handwriting experts can analyse personality traits, all artists, especially in their drawing, have personal mannerisms. It is often interesting to see by the direction of shading which artists are left- or right-handed, for instance. This characteristic was further exploited in the *Impressionist* artist Degas' use of *pastel*, and more so in Monet's late work, although it comes into most prominence with *Abstract Expressionism*.

■ *Links: Abstract Expressionism, automatism, gestural painting, Impressionism.*
■ *Formal elements:* line.

automatism/automatic writing: a spontaneous technique of painting and writing without conscious thought, as a way of reaching the subconscious beneath. First used in an art context by *Dada* artists, experiments with automatic writing were important to the later *Surrealists* and much used by *Abstract Expressionist* artists. Look at Mark Tobey's paintings of 'white writing', in which he uses small lines like handwriting or signatures, e.g. 'Universal Field', 1949, Whitney Museum of American Art, New York.

In theory automatic painting is easy enough to do: with a blank surface and a blank mind, your unconscious tells your hand what shapes to make. In practice the conscious mind always overrides any free thought. Take a large sheet of paper and a brush with a single colour, or a big soft pencil and see what happens — it will take several pages before the work becomes truly 'automatic'. These could then be treated as the basis for some careful visual research into different types of abstraction, or an investigation into your own *autographic marks.*

■ *Links: Dada, gestural painting, Surrealism.*
■ *Formal elements:* line, colour, texture.

avant-garde: artistic groups or artistic statements that are ahead of their time and point beyond what already exists and anticipate future trends, often involving *shock* to make their audience think.

■ *When:* first named and noticed in nineteenth-century Paris.
■ *Links: Impressionism, Realism, shock.*

background: term describing that part of a painting which appears to be behind the central area of attention. In traditional *composition* this is an area with little interest of its own; it merely serves to focus the eye on the key areas. From *Impressionism* onwards, particularly Monet's late water lilies begun in the 1890s, paintings lose the distinction between background, *midground* and *foreground* to become an all-over field of vision. *Cubism* made no distinction between the object painted and the space that surrounded it, e.g. Picasso's 'Ma Jolie', 1911–12, Museum of Modern Art, New York; a process that could be said to reach a high point with *Abstract Expressionism*, e.g. Jackson Pollock's 'Number 1', 1948, Museum of Modern Art, New York, or Barnett Newman's 'vir Heroicus Sublimus', 1950–51, Museum of Modern Art, New York, a vast horizontal red canvas of 2.42 by 5.41 metres with vertical stripes.

■ *Links:* compare the traditional use of the background, e.g. Rembrandt's 'Portrait of Magaretha de Geer', 1661, National Gallery London, where the woman is the centre and foreground of the painting, the background just a prop, to de Kooning's 'Woman' series, e.g. 'Woman 1', 1950–52, Museum of Modern Art, New York, where the woman is foreground, mid- and background all at the same time.

■ *Formal elements: colour* — think of the different properties of colour in creating depth.

Baroque: the Baroque was both a style and a period of time. Its initial purpose was to express the power of the Catholic church in great splendour. This was in response to the rise of the more rational Protestantism (an approach to Christianity which depended on interpreting the word of God, rather than the depiction of religious beliefs through visual images). Baroque art was characterised by strong movement, dramatic imagery, powerful lighting and rich colours, i.e. great visual excitement and the illustration of power. It emphasised balance in the separate parts in order to create a harmonious whole.

■ *When:* Europe, 1600 to late 1700s.

■ *Who:* Gianlorenzo Bernini, architect, sculptor, painter and set designer, the major artist of seventeenth-century Rome (the initial centre of Baroque art), Michelangelo Caravaggio, Annibale Carracci, Peter Paul Rubens, e.g. 'Samson and Delilah', 1609, National Gallery, London.

■ *Links: Mannerism, Renaissance.* Compare Baroque sculpture with painting, e.g. Bernini's 'The Ecstasy of St Teresa', 1645, San Maria della Vittoria, Rome. The carved marble gives an astonishing illusion of rippling cloth as the saint receives the arrow of religious ecstasy. Caravaggio's 'Martyrdom of St Matthew', 1600, in the Contarelli Chapel, San Luigi dei Francesi, Rome, is a painting full of great skill, e.g. the use of *illusion, foreshortening* and **chiaroscuro**; the swirling illustration of great violence, movement and emotion. Baroque art, although more theatrical, developed after the decline of the Renaissance. For a complete contrast look at later *Neo-classical* painting, e.g. David's 'Oath of the Horatii', 1784, Musée du Louvre, Paris. Compare Caravaggio, Bernini and David for good examples of what theatrical means in the Baroque context.

■ *Formal elements:* tone — the use of powerful light from a single source, showing deep shadow, intense highlights and clear breaks between light and dark.

bas relief: see *relief.*

Bauhaus: a school of art and design founded in Germany in 1919 by the architect Walter Gropius. The school moved to Dessau in 1925, into buildings designed by Gropius, characterised by flat white planes of concrete, huge industrial-looking windows, balconies and flat roofs. Important not only for the quality of industrial design work, but also for the concept that art, design and craft were equally relevant and should be studied together. In their first year, students had to investigate all the forms of making and design — this system is still in use in the foundation course of British art schools. In its last years, the Bauhaus was dominated by architecture; it was closed by the Nazis in 1933.

Early Bauhaus work was *Expressionist,* e.g. 'Cathedral of Socialism', Lionel Feininger, 1919, the first woodcut illustrating the aims of the new school, which showed a Gothic-style cathedral and was similar in intention to work by *Der Blaue Reiter.* Once the school moved to Dessau, the characteristic machine age Bauhaus design appears, much influenced by *De Stijl.* Van Doesburg taught there briefly and was partly responsible for the dramatic change from Expressionism. Marcel Breuer's tubular steel furniture was first designed in 1925 and based on bicycle handlebars (see *bicycle*). He developed this process, using an unbroken length of tubing, into the cantilever chair, the B32 of 1926. Mies van der Rohe (who was the last real president of the Bauhaus) remodelled this idea into his famous Barcelona chair of 1928, still manufactured today and used in any fashion shoot that features high style.

Other Bauhaus design included a great deal of innovative graphic work, especially a rounded bold typeface, available on most word processing packages and worth using if studying this period.

■ *When:* Germany, 1919–33.

■ *Who:* almost a roll-call of key early twentieth-century European abstract artists and designers — Josef Albers, Theo van Doesburg, Wassily Kandinsky, Paul Klee, László Moholy-Nagy, Mies van der Rohe.

■ *Links: bicycle, Constructivism, design, De Stijl, Expressionism*. The crisp, machine-like Bauhaus graphics were particularly influential, especially the use of images and block and line within the text. Documenting the change from early expressionist Bauhaus to the industrial design of the later 1920s and making the same sort of changes in your own art could prove very fruitful. Look also at the later work of Josef Albers in America and his 'Homage to the Square' series of experiments with squares and close-toned *colour*.

■ *Formal elements:* pattern and shape.

Ben Day dots/Ben Day process: a cheap industrial printing process used in magazines and newspapers, named after Benjamin Day, an American printer. The image is printed using a pattern of dots. Each dot has a different density, creating a half-toned image, which can be used for both colour and black and white images.

■ *Links: complementary colours, divisionism, Pop art*. It was this mass media process that Roy Lichtenstein turned into art in his famous paintings from comics. For instance 'Wham', 1963, Tate Modern, London, is painted entirely in single colour dots. It depicts a small comic strip image of a plane shooting down another plane and has been blown up into a painting that is 172 cm by 406 cm. Look at other uses of dots, for example Seurat and *divisionism*. What are the artists' intentions? Can you use both in your work and which is most appropriate?

■ *Formal elements:* tone (in particular this method reduces tone to areas of distinct contrast), pattern — seen through a magnifying glass, the Ben Day dots are just abstract patterns that resolve into an image from a distance.

bicycle: there are a surprising number of references to bicycles in the history of *Modernist* art. Maurice Vlaminck, the *Fauvist*, was a professional and champion cyclist; Picasso put a bicycle saddle and handlebars together to make a bull's head (see *found objects* and *Cubism*). When Marcel Breuer, the Bauhaus designer and teacher, moved to Dessau he bought a racing bicycle and was inspired by its handlebars to invent his tubular steel furniture, e.g. the Wassily chair, 1925, still in production (see *Bauhaus*). One of the most important pre-*Conceptual art* sculptures was Duchamp's first *ready-made*, 1912, in which he mounted a bicycle wheel on a stool to produce a ready-made sculpture. Willem de Kooning's

'Woman and a Bicycle', 1952–53, Whitney Museum of American Art, New York, shows them both in huge *Abstract Expressionist, gestural* brushstrokes. Famously, in the same period, Jackson Pollock is supposed to have ridden a bike across one of his canvases.

■ *Links: Bauhaus, found objects, ready-made.* The bicycle in modern art would make an interesting starting point for a coursework contextual study. Alternatively, use your study of one form of transport to research another, e.g. the car, the skateboard, or the aeroplane. See James Rosenquist's 'F1–11', 1965, Private Collection, New York, a 26.2 metres long painting featuring the newly-arrived fighter plane.

Although they are very difficult to draw in themselves, a better approach to bicycles would be to base your visual research on the effects of riding one. Peter Lanyon, the British landscape artist, made many paintings about the sensations of flying in a glider, e.g. 'Soaring Flight', 1960, Arts Council Collection, which show the landscape from above and the effects of wind speed, changing light and multiple viewpoints. You could document a bicycle ride in the same manner, making use of collage, precise drawings, maps and the different sensations produced during the journey.

Blaue Reiter, Der: (The Blue Rider) an artists' association that turned away from academic painting and the quasi-scientific aims of *Impressionism* and instead attempted to express the spiritual in art. An important book for early *abstract* art was published by Kandinsky in 1912 (*The Art of Spiritual Harmony*, translated into English in 1914). The members of the group had a loose set of aims, generally summed up by *Expressionism* and a move towards the abstract and spiritual. *Der Blaue Reiter* was also the title of a magazine containing essays about European and African art, first published by Wassily Kandinsky and Franz Marc in 1912.

■ *When:* Munich, Germany, 1911–14.

■ *Who:* Lyonel Feininger, Wassily Kandinsky, Auguste Macke, Franz Marc, Gabrielle Münter.

■ *Links: Bauhaus, Die Brücke, Expressionism.* Der Blaue Reiter was a more intellectual, visually softer group than *Die Brücke* but was linked to them in the belief that an art work could no longer be an illusionistic depiction of reality; reality had become so complex that it was the function of art to look beneath the surface. Art should 'no longer reproduce the visible, but make things visible' (Paul Klee). The art of members of Der Blaue Reiter showed different approaches to abstraction. Kandinsky painted some of the early, completely abstract paintings, e.g. 'Improvisation no. 19', 1911, from the Stadtische Galerie im Lenbachaus, Munich, trying to recreate the inner spiritual reality that traditional painting does not reach. This spirituality of Der Blaue Reiter reappeared in the first Expressionist years of the *Bauhaus*.

b

Franz Marc's images of animals, horses especially, are not just representations of semi-abstract animal life. For example in 'Little Yellow Horse', 1912, Staatsgallerie, Stuttgart, these animals are symbols of the natural state, of purity. They are creation itself since they live in harmony with nature. For Marc, yellow symbolises female, blue masculinity and red matter. Try assigning characteristics or even characters to the use of pure *colour* in your work. Will these qualities affect the way the colour is applied, or its relationship with the colour next to it? Marc's methods have strong links to Delaunay's use of colour in his paintings of the Eiffel Tower (see *Cubism*).

■ *Formal elements:* colour (Franz Marc), pattern (Kandinsky).

Brit art: see *YBAs*.

bronze: an alloy of copper and tin that is harder and more durable than brass and has been used since ancient Greek times for *casting sculpture*. It develops an attractive *patina* with age.

■ *Links: casting, patina, sculpture.*

Brücke, Die: (The Bridge) group of *Expressionist* artists in Dresden, Germany, formed to make art that rebelled against German academic conventions, art that was even more subjective than *Fauvism*. Die Brücke developed a group style based on *primitivism*, and like the earlier *Impressionists*, their subject matter was nature. Although they were not really dedicated ***plein air*** artists, they made sketches outside that were then worked up in the studio, e.g. Erich Heckel, 'Woodland Pool', 1910, Staatsgallerie Moderner Kunst, Munich. The natural world was the starting point for the content of their paintings. The work of Die Brücke artists featured flat areas of intense colour, with heavy outlines much influenced by medieval *woodcuts*, *Post-Impressionism* and *African art*, e.g. Kirchner's 'Self Portrait with Model', 1910, Kunsthalle, Hamburg, with its intense bands of orange and blue against a red background, the figures' faces reduced to lines and curves.

■ *When:* Dresden Germany, 1905–13.

■ *Who:* Erich Heckel, Karl Schmitt-Rottluff, Ernst Kirchner.

■ *Links: Bauhaus, Der Blaue Reiter, Expressionism.* The other half of the German Expressionist art movement, Die Brücke were more aggressively primitive than *Der Blaue Reiter*. To demonstrate the intentions behind Expressionism, try comparing them with the Impressionist search for optical truth. The meaning of Die Brücke painting, unlike Impressionism, does not lie in the objective world as perceived, but in the way in which the artist has painted it: 'The total transposition of a personal idea into a work' (Kirchner).

Look at *Post-Impressionism*. The intense colour comes from van Gogh especially, and Die Brücke's interest in non-European art owes a great deal to Gauguin. Kirchner's characteristic images of the city, e.g. 'Five Women in the

b

Street', 1913, Wallraf-Richartz Museum, Cologne, demonstrate a growing awareness of the notions of alienation. European art from Manet's 'Music in the Tuileries Gardens', 1862, National Gallery, London, onwards, is full of images of the city. It is a theme that is well worth pursuing.

Die Brücke artists were responsible for reintroducing the *woodcut* into the fine art tradition, e.g. Erich Heckel's 'Crouching Woman', 1913. Woodcut is a very expressive and quick medium, not unlike a more powerful and expressive form of lino print. Working with woodcut as a result of an art study on Die Brücke would be a logical way to proceed.

■ *Formal element:* colour and form are the key expressive elements; local colour was not used.

brush: a tool made of bristles or hair set into a handle in order to apply paint to a surface. It was probably invented in the Stone Age. Although the majority of brushes made since the 1960s contain synthetic fibres, their design is still based on traditional materials. Each type of brush is designed for a specific function: watercolour brushes, for instance, have short black handles and long pointed hairs. Because the amount of material they manipulate is small, generally the area they need to cover is equally small and the majority of hand movements are from the fingers rather than the wrist or shoulder. The best watercolour brushes are called sables, fine haired, tapered with a pointed end. Good brushes can be expensive and the very best are Kolinsky sable made from the tail of the kolinsky or Siberian mink, which can cost up to £1,500 per pound weight.

Oil painting brushes are long handled, called brights, flats, rounds and filberts; the best are made from the bristles of eastern European pigs. Brights are broad, flat with a square end, the bristles relatively short, used for thicker paint and short brushstrokes. Flats are longer-bristled versions of brights and are more versatile. A round is a long tapering, pointed brush, a bristle version of a sable and not as good for putting down an area of paint as a flat. The filbert is like a flat but with rounded, rather than squared-off, ends and therefore more use for a generalised area of painting than for painting straight lines.

All these brushes were originally designed for oil paint or watercolour. The slightly different properties of *acrylic* do not demand such high-quality bristles and hairs. Also, the constant dipping in water and the tendency of polymer paints to clog the root end of the brush damages the very best quality brushes.

● Brush care: try to use the best quality brushes you can afford and look after them properly. Wash all brushes immediately after use; never leave them standing bristles-down in water or another *medium*. Wash brushes under running water, using soap or washing-up liquid; either leave to dry with the bristles up in a jar, or, if they belong to you (and that is the best way to get brushes to do what you want), dry them and keep them in a brush wallet, not stuffed in the bottom of your folder.

b

■ *Links:* different brushes produce different effects, and a painter's brushwork is as personal as a signature (see *autographic mark*) — think of van Gogh's thick paint with each stroke of the brush still visible. Matisse, for instance, worked with long bamboo canes stuck to his brushes to produce those elegant curving lines. It is worth experimenting with methods and materials, and keeping a record of the results.

In contrast, the champion of smooth brushwork, where the paint is so blended that the brushstroke is invisible, is the *Neo-classical* artist, Ingres, e.g. 'Madame Moitessier', 1856, National Gallery, London. Contrast this with the open brushwork (where each stroke of the bristle is evident) of *Impressionism*, only 13 years later, e.g. Monet's 'La Grenouillere', 1869, National Gallery, London, where light is not beautifully modulated but shown in individual sweeps of the brush. Or *Abstract Expressionism*, where the paint is poured rather than brushed on.

Some artists' work changes as they use other brushes — for instance, early Lucian Freud paintings were painted with a sable brush, e.g. 'Girl with a White Dog', 1950, Tate Britain. Freud had been studying Ingres and the paint is very smooth, but for his later paintings, e.g. 'Woman Smiling', 1958–59, Private Collection, he had looked at Frans Hals and Titian and used a bristle brush. Here the painterliness of increasingly thick paint helps to indicate the qualities of actual flesh.

Byzantine art: Christian art from the eastern half of the Roman Empire. The important element was not the personality of the artist but instruction of the faithful viewer. Byzantine art was highly stylised — it repeated the same basic images in the same format and made constant representations of the human figure. Byzantine art was originally derived via Roman art from the Greeks, but in its eastern form it was two-dimensional, featuring surface pattern rather than, for instance, the later *Renaissance* use of *tone* to create pictorial depth.

The vehicles for Byzantine art were largely *fresco, mosaic,* illuminated manuscript and the *icon.* It is the mosaics that are probably the most well-known, e.g. the mosaics in the dome of Hagia Sophia, 885, Thessaloniki, Greece, which show the apostles dressed in classical togas, although the folds are now depicted as golden lines that make zigzag patterns in flat shapes across their bodies. They stand on green and white curved shapes, perhaps hills, against a gold background, and are the same height as the trees around them. This is not naturalism, but the telling of a well-known story with the key elements selected and emphasised. It was against these stylised forms of Byzantine art that the very first steps were taken towards the naturalism that characterised the *Renaissance,* e.g. Duccio's 'Virgin and Child', before 1308, National Gallery, London, the central panel of a *triptych.* The Virgin has the characteristic long Roman nose of Byzantine *icons* and the rightwards tilt of the head. She holds her hands in the predictably formal, stylised manner, but the gestures of the Christ child as he tugs at her clothes, and the depth in the folds of cloth beneath her hands, all point forwards to something new.

■ *When:* AD 330–1453, although this style of art certainly predated Emperor Constantine founding this part of the Empire in 330, and lasted after the fall of Constantinople (formerly known as Byzantion, now called Istanbul) in 1453.

■ *Links:* *classical, icon, mosaic, Renaissance.*

camera obscura: a pinhole-type camera that projects an image through a small hole, or lens, onto a surface so that it can be traced upside down. It was used from the sixteenth century to help with studying the perspective of constructions, portraits and proportions and general accuracy in drawing. You can tell drawings that have used a *camera obscura*, because they will be small. Only small pieces of paper can fit in the device, and very careful, precise line drawings around the edges of what can be traced have been used. These drawings also favour a panoramic composition. Both Canaletto and Vermeer are known to have used something similar.

■ *Links:* David Hockney has written a large book — *Secret Knowledge* (2000) Thames and Hudson — on the disputed role of this device, showing how the painting of *perspective* changed after about 1400. It might be worth creating a similar machine yourself and using it to compare different approaches to representing a view of a room, or a landscape, for example.

■ *Formal elements:* line, tone (the role of light is crucial).

canvas: has two different meanings. The first one is the woven cotton or linen material which is stretched over a wooden armature frame, or stretcher, on which the artist paints. Stretched material has been a support for paint since the fifteenth century, although preparing it and making the stretcher takes longer than some other methods. Canvas now comes in two basic materials: linen which is naturally a light brown colour; and cotton which is usually white, cheaper, often easier to find, but does not last as long. These materials come in different grades and weights — the finer the weave, the smoother the surface to paint on and therefore the finer the quality of brushwork that can be used. The standard cotton canvas is usually cotton duck at 410 gsm and linen is either fine, or superfine grade. Canvas is prepared either by painting with cold water glue *size* (or, as in the days of commercial artists' studios, size made from rabbit skin) to leave the colour of the canvas unaffected, or by priming the surface with a suitable white or mid-coloured *ground*. The second meaning of canvas refers to the whole work as a 'canvas'.

■ *Links:* *Abstract Expressionism, gestural painting.* Artists have different approaches to how they use canvas. Francis Bacon always painted on the reverse, unpainted, side of already primed linen canvas because he wanted to use the brown ground but needed the priming on the other side to stop too much paint being absorbed. Jackson Pollock did not stretch his canvas over a stretcher at all but dripped his paint onto canvas tacked directly onto the floor, so that his paintings reflected the full sweep of his arm.

cartoon: a term that has two main meanings. The first one is for the drawing on paper of the main forms of a *composition* to be used in a large work, sometimes for a tapestry or painting, generally for a *fresco*, although cartoons were important later in the creation of stained glass, and can be used in making *mosaics*.

■ *When:* until the fifteenth century fresco designs were sketched freehand onto the wet plaster. From this period onwards, the basic drawing was made full-size on strong paper and the part needed for that day would be torn off or cut into sections (called a *giornate*) and placed against the wall. The lines on the drawing were transferred to the wet plaster, either by cutting through the paper, or by 'pouncing', in which small holes were pricked through the paper along the drawn lines and fine powder was then rubbed or blown through the holes to show the lines to be worked on. Cartoons could also be used for easel painting; Leonardo's 'Virgin and Child with St Anne and the Infant St John', *c.* 1500, National Gallery, London was made as a cartoon for a large panel painting, but never actually used. You can tell this because there are no holes pricked through the paper.

Nowadays, the word 'cartoon' means humorous or satirical images of a topical event, usually appearing in a magazine or newspaper. Apparently the first use of this version dates from 1843, when the humorous magazine *Punch* entered a drawing of this style into a serious competition to find decorations for the newly rebuilt Houses of Parliament. The meaning of the term has developed, particularly since the invention of animated drawings, e.g. Walt Disney films, *The Simpsons*, etc. Another version of cartoon is the comic strip, consisting of a series of drawings in a horizontal repeated frame format. The term is also applied to caricatures and line drawings of imaginary figures, although such images demand particular skills. These are ways of working that should be used carefully in an examination setting. It is important that students can show the development of their own visual language, generally by observation drawing — not always possible with cartoons, which tend to depend on pastiche and copying the style of other cartoonists. *Pop art*, however, and Roy Lichtenstein in particular, used the language of comics to make powerful contemporary imagery — see 'As I opened Fire…', 1964, Stedelik Museum, Amsterdam. Lichtenstein works in the *fine art* tradition, using art to analyse and comment on ordinary life. The flat brightness of the colour and the use of black outlines to create quickly recognisable imagery was a reaction to the painterly spontaneity of the previous *Abstract Expressionists* and the carefully blended tones of the typical figure painting that came before *Modernism*.

■ *Links: drawing, fresco, Pop art, Renaissance.*

■ *Formal elements:* line.

carving: the reductive method by which an unformed block of material such as stone, wood or plaster (plaster can be carved once it has been cast into suitable block) is shaped by removing the material using tools such as chisels and mallets. The marks of the tools can be left to show the presence of the artist or smoothed away to produce a perfect surface that can mimic human flesh.

■ *Links: assemblage, casting, modelling, sculpture.* Contrast the various surfaces of Rodin's 'The Kiss', 1901–04, Tate Modern, London, where the marble has both smoothly polished human limbs and hair, and a plinth which bears the marks of the carver's chisels.

■ *Formal elements:* form, texture.

casting: the process of sculpting in which a mould is made from a solid form and the cast is made by pouring a liquid *medium,* e.g. bronze, plaster, wax, into the hollow mould. It is possible to make casts in multiples if the mould can be taken apart (e.g. two plaster halves). If not, the casting will be a one-off, e.g. the clay mould of a fist for a plaster cast can only be used once. Casting marks can often be seen in multiple versions.

■ *Links: bronze, sculpture.* Rachel Whiteread's 'House', the largest cast art object ever made (see *YBAs*).

■ *Formal elements:* form, texture.

ceramics: a hard, breakable material made by firing clay, it is a term that covers all forms of pottery. The British, like the Japanese, have a long tradition of producing fine ceramics, particularly in places like St Ives in Cornwall.

■ *Links:* look at the work of Bernard Leach or Lucy Rie.

■ *Formal elements:* all.

charcoal: charred twigs of willow that have been heated without the presence of air. Charcoal comes in varying grades of thickness, but all are equally black — the harder you press, the darker the mark. Thin sticks of charcoal are particularly useful for quick line drawings, and larger sticks (called scene painter's sticks) can be used to create large areas of varying *tone,* using the white of the paper or white chalk to make highlights. Charcoal's virtue is its cheapness and speed of use; its drawback for examination purposes is that it does not keep very well. In a sketchbook it will rub off on the facing page and quickly fill the rest of the book with greyness. Larger, loose drawings are equally difficult to keep clean, as all the careful modulations will gradually fade and smudge away. Fixatives do exist, but they are expensive and do not work that well.

■ *Formal elements:* line — charcoal is supreme for drawing tone to create form.

chiaroscuro: a technique used in painting since the sixteenth century, in which a strong, dramatic contrast of light and dark masses is used to create form.

■ *Who:* the great master of this technique was Michelangelo Caravaggio, the late sixteenth century *Baroque* Italian artist, who famously killed a man in Rome in an argument over a tennis match, attacked a judge in Naples, was knifed in a brothel and died chasing a boat that had taken all his belongings. His paintings are equally dramatic — look at 'The Supper at Emmaus', 1601, National Gallery, London, in which the strong light from the left creates deep shadows and strong highlights; a great sense of drama and importance, with solid figures and almost sculptural cloth.

■ *Links:* the *Baroque*, and *Impressionism* as a contrast.

■ *Formal elements:* tone.

cinquecento: the sixteenth century, especially with reference to Italian art, architecture and literature.

Classical/classicism/classic: three terms, each with a slightly different meaning. Classical with a capital 'C' means the Classical era in Ancient Greece, which ran from about 490 BC to the unification of the Greek city states by Philip of Macedon in 338 BC. This was the period in which art, and sculpture in particular, moved towards a striking naturalism based on the close study of human proportions — for example, the sculpture of a single, standing nude made by the fifth-century Greek sculptor Polycleitos, the 'Doryphorus' or 'Spear Bearer', which we only know from the later Roman copy now in the Museo Archeologico Nazionale, Naples. The figure is moving forward so that his weight is put onto his right leg. His left hand holds the spear and his head is turned slightly to the right. This arrangement of the figure, the slight turning of the body, is called **contrapposto**, and is the major element in creating the lifelike naturalism that characterises the Classical period. Polycleitos was responsible for drawing up rules for the ideal male beauty, as exemplified in the 'Spear Bearer'. His canon (rule or law) depended on the basic principles of mathematical proportion, the ratio of each part of the body to all the other parts in order, from the smallest to the whole — i.e. from one finger to the next, of all the fingers to the hand, and so on. This principle leads logically to the relationship of man to his surroundings, i.e. 'man is the measure of all things' (Protagoras, ?485–?411 BC, Greek philosopher). Greek architecture had an equal, if not greater, effect on later cultures, and the rules of proportion were equally important in Classical architecture. The most characteristic unit of Greek architecture was the column, of which there were three basic styles, or orders: Doric, Ionic and Corinthian. Each order of column had different widths and decorative elements at the top. The width of the column was the unit of proportion for the rest of the building. This results in buildings that are harmonious, with each part relating to the whole. The standard type of Classical architecture is the temple, the most recognisable element of which is the pedimented portico, the main covered entrance. This consisted of a row of columns in the centre of the façade (or front) of the building, supporting a triangular pediment or roof structure, usually separate from the rest of the building. The most famous example of Classical architecture is the Parthenon in Athens, 447–438 BC. It was built in the Doric order as a temple to Athena, goddess of wisdom. Sections of the sculptural decorations from the Parthenon are currently in the British Museum, London.

Classicism means art that is derived from a study of Greek and Roman art and architecture, e.g. *Neo-classicism*. Art of this type, sometimes confusingly called classical with a small 'c', has certain characteristics that its makers will have taken from the past and which can be contrasted with, for instance, *Romanticism*. The return to classicism was the essential component of the *Renaissance*, and became central for most art forms from the mid-eighteenth century onwards. Generally, art containing classical features looks back to Ancient Greece and Rome as a perfect time, so this search for the ideal will be contained in the work. In painting and sculpture this is often represented by symmetrical or harmonious composition (all the elements are balanced), idealised figures (not recognisably individuals), and figures which are either naked or wearing some sort of toga or floating drapery, revealing the shape of the body underneath, e.g. Piero della Francesca's 'Baptism of Christ', 1445, National Gallery, London. In architecture, the principles of classicism have been applied from the Renaissance onwards, based on the writings of the Roman architect Vitruvius. The design of neo-classical buildings, from about the 1750s, was part of a general desire to return to the virtues of ancient Roman laws and reason. The buildings from this period are solid and plain, e.g. Chiswick House, 1725, London, built by Lord Burlington. This is a symmetrical building with pedimented porticoes dominating the flat, undecorated facades — characteristics of classical architecture. Towards the end of the nineteenth century, architecture became heavily decorated and in reaction to this, later *Modernist* architecture featured a return to the underlying principles, e.g. Le Corbusier's Villa Savoye, 1928–31, France, which is a symmetrical white rectangular box apparently supported by thin columns — a reworking of the classical prototype.

The third term 'classic' means something that is seen as the best of its kind or serving as a standard or model — a classic car for example.

■ *Links: Gothic, Nazi art, Neo-classicism, Renaissance, Romanticism.*

Cloisonnism/cloisonnisme: a late nineteenth-century style of painting, in which flat areas of strong colour are surrounded by line. This method looks similar to the areas of colour in stained-glass windows.

■ *Who:* developed by Émile Bernard, e.g. 'Picking Apples', 1890, Musée des Beaux-Arts de Nantes, France; Paul Gauguin and the *Nabis* group.
■ *Links: Nabis, Post-Impressionism.*
■ *Formal elements:* colour, pattern.

collage: a method of creating a picture using photographs, news cuttings and pieces of printed paper stuck onto a flat surface to represent the three-dimensional. It was first developed as an art form by the *Cubist* artists Picasso and Braque in 1912. Collage can, unlike *montage*, involve images made especially for the work. Collage has two important strands still relevant today; it was the first use of non-*fine art* materials in an art setting, a process that has developed ever since, from *Dada* and *Surrealism* to *Pop art* and *Brit art*, and is still being explored today. Second, like the basic idea behind Cubism itself, a collage assumes that the world is complex and cannot be represented by a single image — many contrasting images and methods are needed. Much late twentieth-century art is presented in the form of a collection, 'a palette of objects' as Robert Rauschenberg, the American Pop artist, called it, e.g. Damien Hirst's 'Pharmacy', 1992, Tate Modern, London. The interest is in the relationship of these objects to themselves, to the whole artwork and to the previous history of art.

■ *Links: Cubism, Junk art, montage, Pop art, Surrealism* and Kurt Schwitters, whose *Merz* collages, made from ordinary objects found lying around, are often quoted by later artists as being influential. Collage has been interpreted in many different ways — for instance work that is entirely made from *found objects*, i.e. Rauschenberg (see *Pop art*) or Joseph Cornell's strange boxes, e.g. 'Untitled (the Hotel Eden)' 1945, National Gallery of Canada, Ottowa, which has a parrot, a strange scientific device and a ball, amongst other things, collected together in a small display box, making strong links to dreams, *narrative* and Surrealism. Try looking at Rauschenberg's silk-screen paintings, e.g. 'Skyway', 1964, Dallas Museum of Art, USA (see *silk-screen*). Rauschenberg said that his imagery has the sense of switching from one television channel to another, or flicking through a magazine: 'I was bombarded with television sets and magazines, by the excess of the world, I thought that an honest work should incorporate all those elements, which were and are a reality'.

Remember, though, that your work journal must describe the progress of your understanding and display your growing visual language and *craft*. It would not be enough solely to present a few pages torn from a newspaper and a stuffed goat to get the grades that such an interesting collage might deserve.
■ *Formal element:* colour, pattern, texture.

colour: the sensation produced on the eye by rays of light emanating from an object. It is one of the *formal elements* that must be analysed when making *annotations* and therefore part of any analysis you make when creating your own art, e.g. colour studies in a *still life*, flesh tones in figure studies. Colour is an integral part of art and design and therefore students should be able to demonstrate a working knowledge of colour systems. The *work journal* is a good place to develop this. In painting terms, *local colour* is the actual, or true, colour of an object. *Tonal colour* is the effect of light upon the object. Artists sometimes reduce this to monochrome (i.e. shades of black, grey and white) in their drawing or reproduce it by modulation of colour, which is the passage from one colour to another, either through blending, so that the change is hardly visible, or by careful arrangement of similar *hues*. The visible spectrum, white light, is made up of seven main rays which have different wavelengths; these can be seen when dispersed by a prism. The colours of the rainbow range from violet, which has the highest frequency and shortest wavelength, to red with the lowest frequency and longest wavelength. These give the familiar properties ascribed to 'warm' and 'cold' colours, i.e. red appears to be in front of the *picture plane* and blue appears to recede behind it.

Academic art from the *Renaissance* to the nineteenth century made a distinction between colour and *line* (***colore*** and ***disegno***). The technique of using line was considered to be more important than that of colour. Colours were obtained by grinding pigments and were used to reproduce the colours of nature, a process requiring less skill than drawing. However, *Modernist* artists from *Impressionism* onwards stressed the role of colour as fundamentally important to the process of making art. Van Gogh said that 'colour expresses something by itself'.

■ *Links: additive mixing, aerial perspective, Colour Field Painting, divisionism, Expressionism, hue, optical mixing, saturation, subtractive mixing, tonal colour.*

It is worth looking at art made before *Impressionism* as well; for example *Romanticism*, and Delacroix in particular, e.g. 'The Death of Sardanapulus' 1827, Musée du Louvre , Paris, in which the bored and sated king, who is about to die, lies on a vast red bed and watches as those around him are killed. Colour also has obvious symbolic roles within art — the Virgin Mary's robe is always blue, for example. This is for a variety of reasons. Lapis lazuli, the blue mineral pigment from which ultramarine, the colour used in her robe, was made, was the most expensive of pigments, even more so than gold, and therefore only used for the most important characters. The use of ultramarine not only displayed the wealth of the donor (the person or institution that commissioned the painting), but also made the painting a virtuous object in itself, and, by association, made the owner and the viewer virtuous. As the late mediaeval artist Cenino Cennini wrote in 1390, 'Ultramarine blue is a colour illustrious, beautiful, and most perfect, beyond all other colours.' Blue has, of course, a range of symbolic associations that also make it suitable for the Virgin's clothing — with heaven, spirituality, humility and the ocean. For the use of red, look at 'The Family of Darius',1573, by Paolo Veronese in the National Gallery, London, in which the wife of the defeated Persian Emperor pleads with Alexander the Great for her life, but to the wrong man. She has mistakenly presumed that a red cloak indicates Alexander, who, with this victory, has become the most important man in the world, and so logically should be wearing the strongest colour.

De Stijl, like many other early twentieth-century art movements, nominated spiritual characteristics to each of the primary colours. Wassily Kandinsky, the early twentieth-century Russian artist, one of the founders of the *Bauhaus*, had synaesthesia, a condition in which he responded to sound, especially music, by seeing or feeling specific colours. 'Colour is a power which directly influences the soul. Colour is the keyboard, the eyes are the hammers, the soul is the piano with many strings.' His paintings try to exploit this connection, e.g. 'Swinging', 1925, Tate Modern, London, a picture that uses a visual language of wavy lines and areas of colour that have as much to with calligraphy (hand writing) as the traditional *illusionistic* aims of art.

Colour Field Painting: a trend in *Abstract Expressionism* in which a *colour* covers the whole surface, or field, of the canvas without any other obvious expression in the painting. Colour Field Paintings were characterised by large areas of close tones and similar intensity, large size and simple *composition.* This led to a division between *gestural painting* and Colour Field.

■ *When:* chiefly in the 1960s.

■ *Links:* also led to *Minimalism* and *Op art.* Barnett Newman, 'Adam', 1951, Tate Modern, London, and Mark Rothko, 'Black and Maroon', 1958, Tate Modern, London, or in fact the whole Rothko Room at Tate Modern, in which huge dark canvases create a new form of grandeur and spiritual contemplation.

■ *Formal elements:* colour, pattern.

combine painting: the artist Robert Rauschenberg used *junk* and *found objects* to create what he called 'combines' of painting, sculpture and photographic images. Unlike the *Surrealists*, who used the random meeting of objects to release the subconscious, Rauschenberg did not investigate himself through his art: 'I don't mess around with my subconscious, I try to keep wide awake'. Although they also owe something to Duchamp's *ready-mades*, the combines are *formalist* works concerned, like *Abstract Expressionism*, with the quality and arrangement of elements within a piece of art. In contrast to them, though, his art interacted with the world around him — it wasn't restricted to the studio. It was for this reason that Rauschenberg's work started to contain more and more references to the media and images used in advertising.

■ *When:* the late 1950s in America. Probably the first combine painting was 'Bed', 1955, oil and pencil on pillow, quilt and sheet on wood supports, Museum of Modern Art, New York — the artist covered his bedding with paint when he ran out of canvas. The most famous is probably 'Monogram', 1955–59, Moderna Museum, Stockholm, a stuffed angora goat with a car tyre around its middle standing on a square, image-covered board that almost acts like the traditional sculptural plinth. This image has probably lasted because of its combination of surprise (or *shock*) with the familiar, i.e. a pet (as a child, Rauschenberg had a pet goat whose death affected him a great deal). Rauschenberg stopped making combines in 1962 and began to concentrate on two-dimensional imagery using silk screen and advertising images, e.g. 'Skyway', 1964, Dallas Museum of Art — a collaged silk screen image featuring President Kennedy, astronauts, street signs and a painting of Rubens' 'Venus', in a slightly grid-like structure.

Rauschenberg's rule for his own art, 'the work had to look at least as interesting as anything that was going on outside the window', is an idea that could be applied to any installation or combine that you might want to create. The combination of objects familiar to you with public imagery (e.g. advertising) as shown in 'Monogram' is full of possibilities, but make sure that you ground any work securely in the history of art, starting with *Cubist* collage, and in basic observation work.

■ *Links: Abstract Expressionism, assemblage, collage, Dada, Merz, Pop art, ready-made.*
■ *Formal elements:* form, pattern, texture.

complementary colours: the colours opposite each other on the colour circle or colour triangle which produce white if mixed *additively,* and black if mixed *subtractively*: red–green, blue–orange, yellow–violet. With complementary *contrast* the effects of the colour are intensified; for example, mix blue and yellow to get green, the complementary colour of red. The opposite of complementary colours, i.e. those next to each other, e.g. red/orange, are called analogous.

■ *Links: optical mixing, secondary colours, divisionism* in which the *Neo-Impressionist* artists, Georges Seurat and Paul Signac, used small dots of contrasting colour to produce stronger effects than if the colours had been mixed on the *palette*. Look at 'La Grande Jatte' by Georges Seurat, 1884–46, Art Institute of Chicago.
■ *Formal elements:* colour.

composition: the arrangement of the formal structure of a work of art. The ordering principles of different types of art will vary according to style and materials used. Principles of composition can be: relation of colour and form, symmetry/asymmetry, movement/rhythm, etc. Contemporary artists decide the ordering principles of a composition themselves, but in the past artists working for a commission or in a society with strong religious beliefs would have used traditional forms of composition.

■ *When:* working thematically, as most examined work demands that theme should be one of the ordering principles. For example, a work analysing movement would demand a vigorous, probably disjointed, pictorial structure much like Boccioni's 'The City Rises', Museum of Modern Art, New York, 1910. In this *Futurist* work the foreground is dominated by a red horse curving across the canvas, painted with shaking, multicoloured lines and barely held by figures that lean diagonally across the powerful animal. Contrast this with a painting analysing stability, most often found in traditional scenes from Christ's life. To contemporary viewers this was a familiar story, representing their world order, e.g. Masaccio, 'The Holy Trinity', 1427, Santa Maria Novella, Florence.

■ *Links: Futurism, Renaissance.*

Conceptual art: the precursor to Conceptual art was probably Marcel Duchamp (see *Dada*), in particular his *ready-mades*. Artists in America and Europe in the 1960s began to move away from recording individual objects to working entirely with ideas. The key areas of interest for Conceptual artists were the greater importance of communicating an idea than making a permanent object (see *art object*), and the intention behind the work of art and its presentation in a commercial gallery or museum. A classic early Conceptual piece is the word painting by John Baldessari from 1968, a canvas which reads: 'Everything is purged from the painting but the art'.

Conceptual art was a reaction against the growing commercialisation of much postwar art and the concentration on *formalism,* in other words how to paint, not why and what. Conceptual art was the result of a growing realisation that there is more to art than a young, notionally poor, white man in a studio turning out more luxury goods. Twentieth-century artists must also consider the political, economic and cultural system to which their art contributed. For instance, during the Vietnam War and the Civil Rights movement in America, Adrian Piper exhibited art that said it had been withdrawn 'as evidence of the inability of art expression to have meaningful existence under conditions other than those of peace, equality, truth, trust and freedom'.

■ *When:* from the mid-1960s onwards. Conceptual ideas still inform current work, e.g. the *YBAs.*

■ *Who:* in the USA, artists such as Sol LeWitt, John Baldessari, Douglas Huebler and Joseph Kosuth. Kosuth wrote two key articles in 1969 ('Art after Philosophy') that asked:

- How important is intention — does what an artist thinks he or she is doing have anything to do with the meaning that we, the viewers, give to what artists actually make?
- What are the limits to existing types of art and other ways of communicating visually?
- Does art appeal to the eye or the mind?

The questions were relevant because they emphasised the importance Kosuth (and subsequently other conceptual artists) gave to the prominence of ideas in art, as opposed to the creation of permanent objects. Visual art merely became the vehicle for the concept — it was the concept that was the point of the whole process.

In the UK, the Art and Language group founder members Terry Atkinson and Mel Baldwin looked carefully at the context in which art was displayed. Like their American colleagues, they made works that featured written texts, but Art and Language took the process a step further and presented long written pieces, both as something to read and as an exhibit in themselves. Is reading an entirely intellectual process? The written page is a visual object as much as the shapes of letters are a route to textual knowledge. Conceptual art's questioning of the role of the gallery and the way in which artists are selected and presented led to, for instance, Mary Kelly's 'Post Partum Document (Documentation III)' 1984, Tate Modern, London, in which she carefully documented her relationship with her growing baby and his understanding of the world, by displaying not only her diary but also his drawings and dirty nappies as evidence of objects made by him.

■ *Links:* *art object*, **Arte Povera**, *Land art, Minimalism, ready-made.* Conceptual art was also important for the eventual acceptance of feminism, photography, *Performance art,* and video and text as possible art works.

Constructivism: an abstract art movement that started in Russia, inspired by *Cubism,* which worked largely in three dimensions with abstract geometrical forms. Constructivist sculpture worked with space rather than mass; artists *assembled* pieces of industrial metal, machined wood, wire, etc., unlike earlier sculptors who carved or modelled unformed material. Also important was the Constructivist belief in 'truth to materials' — that the properties of each material should determine how it was used in a sculpture; wood was best for flat planes, metal for making cylinders and so on.

■ *When:* 1913–1920s, originating in Moscow.

■ *Who:* Naum Gabo, El Lissitzky, Alexander Rodchenko, Vladimir Tatlin, Lyubov Popova.

■ *Links:* see also *assemblage, sculpture* and *Suprematism.* Picasso's 'Guitar' of 1912, Museum of Modern Art, New York.

■ *Formal elements:* form.

contemporary: in everyday use this means from the same period. So the contemporary art of today has been made within the last 10 years or so. The term can also be used in general to mean stylish or to describe art made since 1945, to distinguish it from the Modernist period (which was from about 1850 to the 1960s or 1970s). Contemporary art for artists from a different period is, of course, the work that was being made during their lifetime — for Monet it was the other Impressionists; for Michelangelo it was Raphael and Leonardo.

■ *Links:* modern/modernity, Modernism.

contour: in geography a contour line shows a change in height from sea level; in art, contour shows the outline of a form, either drawn as a line or shown through a contrast in *tone* or *colour*.

■ *Links:* often referred to by examiners as the *turning edge*, and used by them as a guide to a student's ability to represent *form*. In your drawing or painting of a three-dimensional object, have you shown how that object turns away from the eye? Or have you merely drawn a line which looks like a sharp edge?

■ *Formal elements:* tone (in the use of darker tones to make parts of the form seem further away from the eye), colour, form, texture.

contrapposto: the name given by the *Renaissance* to a standing figure pose in which the weight of the body is on one leg so that the whole figure appears to be in motion and twisting slightly against itself.

■ *When: contrapposto* was first evolved in fifth-century Greek sculpture, e.g. the development from the 'Kritios boy', 480 BC, Acropolis Museum, Athens, to the 'Doryphoros' by Polyclitus, first century AD, Imperial Roman copy, Museo Archeologico Nazionale di Napoli , Naples. Sculptors progressively tried to show naturalistic movement (rhythmos) in male nude sculpture. *Contrapposto* was rediscovered in the *Renaissance,* and became one of the defining features for representing figures. Rather than being restricted to single figure sculptures, the term later broadened out to mean any form of twisting person, whether in two or three dimensions, and reached its greatest complexity under the *Mannerists,* who followed Michelangelo, e.g. Bronzino's 'Allegory', 1540, National Gallery, London.

■ *Links:* Baroque, Classical, Mannerist, Renaissance.

Look at Greek and Roman sculpture and how the *contrapposto* pose develops in Renaissance sculpture, e.g. from Donatello's 'St George', Orsanmichele, Florence, to Michelangelo's classical 'David', Academia, Florence, to Titian's painting of Bacchus, in his 'Bacchus and Ariadne', National Gallery, London, or the extraordinary distortions of Michelangelo's nudes on the ceiling of the Sistine Chapel in the Vatican Museum, Rome. The logical approach to exploring this subject would be to pose figures in varying forms of *contrapposto*, starting with the early classical weight on one leg, bent at the knee, and culminating in the full-blown *Mannerist* distortion.

■ *Formal elements:* form.

contrast: a comparison showing noticeable differences, so in painting there are light and dark contrasts, colour contrasts, warm and cold contrasts, complementary contrasts and simultaneous contrasts. In the manipulation of light, e.g. photography, video, contrast means the balance between brightness and darkness — the difference between tones. 'Turning up the contrast' in a work would mean making those different qualities even more obvious.

■ *Formal elements:* tone, colour, pattern, texture.

craft/Crafts: has two meanings, that of the special manual skill needed to make a particular thing well, e.g. painting, sculpture, pottery, weaving, and with a capital 'C' crafts means the applied arts (see *Arts and Crafts movement*). These include book binding, ceramics, glass, furniture, textiles and wallpaper. Remember that there are a series of *endorsements* you can take at AS and A-level which include some of these crafts.

Cubism: the fundamental early twentieth-century art movement that paved the way for every other form of *modern art*. Up until this point the function of art had been to create a recognisable imitation of nature, usually with some particular *narrative* purpose, though more recently for its own sake, e.g. *Impressionism* and *Post-Impressionism*. The pre-Cubist methods for depicting the world were through traditional *perspective*, the careful blending of *colour* to model the form and the use of scale, i.e. *foreshortening* and *composition*. By combining an interest in non-Western art (especially *African* and Iberian masks) that used other methods to describe an idea, and Cézanne's paintings (see *Post-Impressionism*), Cubism abandoned illusionism in painting — the idea that the picture plane was a 'fourth wall' on the world. Strongly influenced by Cézanne, the Cubists made each painting a record of the artist's actual perception of the objects in front of them. Importantly, Picasso and Braque added time as a key element of looking, so that in each Analytical Cubist painting (see below) we can see the front and the back of each object simultaneously. In other words, the painting includes all possible ideas about the subject, not just the limited *Renaissance* version of what it looked like from a frontal static position. For the first time in Western art, the Cubists made art that was not restricted to the appearance of the objects it represented; artistic reality could be something other than the visual image that tradition and practice had fixed as the true representation of an object in space.

■ *When:* traditionally the start of Cubism is defined as Picasso's painting, 'Les Demoiselles d'Avignon', 1907, Museum of Modern Art, New York. Cubism is divided into two phases: Analytical Cubism, 1909–11, and Synthetic Cubism,

C

1912–14. An Analytical Cubist painting, e.g. Georges Braque, 'Clarinet and Bottle of Rum on a Mantelpiece', 1911, Tate Modern, London, is characteristically brown and grey, composed of small planes in which the subject matter is only just recognisable.

In a still life of May 1912, 'Still Life with Chair Caning', Musée Picasso, Paris, Picasso glued a printed version of imitation chair caning onto a still life to represent the chair on which the image of the still life he was painting rested. This marked the start of Synthetic Cubism and Cubist *collage* (possibly the most important method Cubism developed). A classic Synthetic Cubist painting, Georges Braque's 'Violin and Pipe', 1913–14, Musée National d'Art Moderne, Centre Georges Pompidou, Paris, shows the still life objects reduced to flat shapes on the picture plane, some cut from newspapers (which describe the approaching war), some drawn. Fake wood wallpaper represents the table, which is tilted vertically to show its contents.

In 1912 Picasso made the first Cubist sculpture, 'Guitar', 1912, Museum of Modern Art, New York, important because it marked the beginning of a new method of making sculpture: *assemblage*. Note that this was happening in Paris, which had been established as the *avant-garde* art capital of the world since the 1850s.

■ *Who:* Pablo Picasso and Georges Braque. Braque had been involved with *Fauvism* before he saw Picasso's 'Les Demoiselles d'Avignon' in 1907. A distinction is made between these two originators of Cubism and the later 'Salon Cubists', La Fresnaye, Gleizes and Metzinger, who took the geometric style and applied it to traditional *narrative* subjects without really changing their underlying approach.

■ *Links:* sources — look at the late paintings of the *Post-Impressionist* painter Cézanne, especially the Bathers series, e.g. 'The Large Bathers', 1894–1905, National Gallery, London. The distortion of Cézanne's figures deeply influenced Picasso's 'Les Demoiselles d'Avignon'. Look also at the importance of non-Western art — visit, for instance, the collections at the British Museum, London, as Picasso visited equivalent collections in Paris. Although Cubism never took the logical step and became *abstract* itself, it was one of the principal sources for abstract art — see, for instance, *Constructivism* or *De Stijl*.

One straightforward approach would be to set up a *still life* and to examine and represent the form of the objects from every angle in an Analytical Cubist manner. This process could be taken a step further by developing a Synthetic Cubist collage on the same subject, or backwards by examining Braque's progression from patches of pure colour in his Fauvist period through to planes of form as a Cubist, then his late still lives, which had a great effect on English artists in the late 1940s and early 1950s, such as Patrick Heron.

Look also at the subject matter of Cubist paintings. Their monochrome palette can make them appear rather dull, but these are not just artistic investigations into the painting of form, as above. This is art about nightlife — many of them depict bottles of alcohol, newspapers referring to politics and other topics of current interest, such as music. Remember that these are paintings made by two increasingly successful young men, at the forefront of the *avant-garde* in the most exciting city in the world. If you were to make art of your own on the same sort of themes, the analytical collage approach would be a good place to start. Document the visual language you develop and make sure that it is initially based on observation work. Look back at Analytical Cubist investigations, of glass for instance, to help with this process.

■ *Formal elements:* Cubism's importance is that it covers all the elements, from the reduction to line by 1912, the pure use of tone in the restricted palette 1907–12, the brighter colour 1912–14, the visual obsession with representing form, derived from Cézanne, that dominates the entire Cubist method. The use of pattern, e.g. the use of 'passage' or short parallel brush strokes to describe the plane of a form, again derived from Cézanne, and texture, that becomes so important with the use of collage.

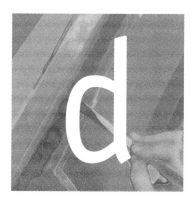

Dada: an influential movement that based its artistic inspiration upon irony and cynicism, born of disillusionment resulting from the carnage of the First World War. It was one of the few self-named artistic groups, although the name is deliberately nonsensical and meaningless, which gives a clue to their intentions. There was no unifying Dada style — the artists used *collage, photomontage,* objects and *ready-mades,* with no concern for materials or craftsmanship. Instead, there were shared attitudes, particularly in questioning the institutionalised art world and its concern with bourgeois values.

■ *When:* Dada began in 1915, during the First World War, with artists rebelling against traditional art values by use of deliberate nonsense and new expressive forms, called 'anti-art', such as *photomontage,* sound poems, *performance* and *shock.* Dadaists blamed the rational, scientific technological approach for the mass slaughter of the First World War. After such appalling senselessness, the only way forward was irrationality and a celebration of the absurd, hence their use of chance in many works.

■ *Who:* Hans Arp, Marcel Duchamp, Max Ernst, Francis Picabia, Man Ray, Kurt Schwitters, Tristan Zara.

■ *When:* 1915–23, Western Europe, especially Switzerland, and New York.

■ *Links:* many Dada artists became involved in the later *Surrealist* movement, which also celebrated the irrational. Dada, especially through Marcel Duchamp (see *ready-made*), influenced the entire direction of twentieth-century art. It was no coincidence, for instance, that the cover of the 'Sensation' catalogue from the 1997 exhibition at the Royal Academy, London, that brought the *YBAs* to fame, featured an iron reminiscent of Man Ray's famous iron with nails studded down the ironing plate ('Gift', 1921). Dadaist use of accident and chance, e.g. *automatic writing,* was later taken up by both the Surrealists and *Abstract Expressionists.*

decalcomania: method where damp paint is splashed onto one surface with a large brush, then a sheet of paper is laid on top and rubbed by hand to transfer most of the paint. It is thought to have been developed by the Spanish *Surrealist*

Óscar Domínguez in Paris. The process is not dissimilar to *monoprinting* and the result is an *organic*, jungle-like surface that can suggest all sorts of possibilities for painting and investigating the subconscious. It was used predominantly by the Surrealist Max Ernst, e.g. 'The Forest', 1927, Tate Modern, London. Ernst also used **frottage** in the same process, where paper is laid over an interestingly textured surface and a rubbing is made.

■ *Links:* automatic writing, Surrealism.

■ *Formal elements:* pattern, texture.

Deposition: see *Pietà*.

design: to plan or make something artistically. You are taking a course in art and design — design in this context includes graphic or three dimensional and requires the creation of either a product suitable for manufacture or a simulated project. Design works by a straightforward process known as 'linear'. A linear design-based process will start with a concept from which a brief is made. For example, consider the concept of children's play: children need to play and they need a space in which to do it; you have to design a poster to advertise a new playground. Alternatively, many people are no longer interested in, or have time for, making their own entertainment and we now prefer to pay for other people to entertain us, most commonly through the medium of television; what then should be the best cover for a television set? Whatever concept and brief you are given or set yourself, you will have to work out the need you are trying to meet.

- Step one is investigation: researching the concept thoroughly, identifying requirements, recording ideas, working from observation, and finding out what others have done in the same area (critical and contextual studies).
- Step two is assimilation: bringing together all the information, making some sort of sense of it, and experimenting.
- Step three is realisation: producing proposals for products.
- Step four is evaluation: at this stage it is crucial that you refer meaningfully to the critical and contextual studies you made earlier, and answer the basic question — did you meet the need you first identified? Importantly, that evaluation then returns you to the start of the process because it should help you review and refine the original concept.

The creative process for design and art are the same, which is why they are categorised together. Each step of the design process is important, so do not forget to include all the different, strange creative ways in which you found your ideas.

De Stijl: or the Style, was the name of a group of mainly Dutch artists and of their magazine, founded in 1917 and edited by Theo van Doesburg. The De Stijl manifesto was published in 1918. Apart from *Cubism*, the other important influences on van Doesburg were Russian *Suprematism* and *Constructivism*. De Stijl aimed to create an easily identifiable visual language, a language that could be defined as geometric, but not symmetrical (that would have demanded an acceptance of the *classical* arrangement of form). The arrangement of contrary forces to create a new harmony, the complete harmonisation of opposites, of positive to negative, line to plane, in life and society as well as in art, was one of the major aims of De Stijl.

Mondrian's paintings represent typical De Stijl — he limited himself to using straight lines and rectangles, with flat blocks of primary colours and black, white and grey. These were seen by him as a metaphor for the invisible, universal relations that lie behind nature and he coined the phrase Neo-Plasticism to describe his style. Rietveld's 'Red Blue Chair', 1917, Stedelijk Museum, Amsterdam, presents the essential parts of a chair as a series of horizontals and verticals, each function or direction painted a different colour; his Schroder house of 1924 in Utrecht took the process further.

De Stijl, or Neo-Plasticism, was a utopian art movement which believed that it could reach artistic purity and therefore total human harmony. So deeply did these artists believe in what they were doing that when, in 1925, van Doesburg started using diagonals in his work, rather than the purely elemental horizontal and vertical, Mondrian left the group and apparently never spoke to him again.

■ *Who:* Piet Mondrian, Theo van Doesburg, Gerrit Rietveld.

■ *When:* 1917–31, Holland.

■ *Links:* the *Bauhaus* (van Doesburg taught at the Bauhaus and was partly responsible for changing its way of thinking), *Cubism, Constructivism, Minimalism* and *Suprematism*. You can observe Mondrian's journey in a series of paintings, starting with observation-based paintings of single trees, e.g. 'Red Tree', 1908, Gemeentemuseum, The Hague, which were influenced by the *Symbolists* and van Gogh (see *Post-Impressionism*), via his first exposure to Cubism (1911–14), e.g. 'The Grey Tree', 1912, Gemeentemuseum, The Hague, through to the characteristic full-blown *abstraction*, e.g. 'Composition', 1929, Solomon R. Guggenheim Museum, New York. This is a process you might wish to follow — you need not work on a single tree, nor should you end up with an imitation Mondrian, but examine carefully the steps that he took. This would also make a sound basis for personal, contextual coursework study.

■ *Formal elements:* colour, form, pattern.

diptych: a painting or carving on a pair of panels, hinged together like a book.

■ *Links:* *polyptych, triptych.* The most famous medieval version in England is the 'Wilton Diptych', 1395, National Gallery, London, which is a portable altarpiece showing Richard II being presented to the Virgin Mary.

Putting two identically sized panels together gives the artist the opportunity of allowing the images to comment on each other. For instance, in Piero della Francesca's double portrait of Battista Sforza and Duke Federico da Montefeltro, 1472, we see the husband and wife looking at each other. She is on the left panel and he is on the right. In fact, she was dead by the time this work was made and the Duke is, as it were, communing with her earthly memory. They are in identical poses and stare directly at each other, not the viewer. On the back of the diptych, further images deepen this idea. Remember that the two doors, or panels, of the diptych were made to close and the paintings on the outside of the closed doors referred to those on the inside, seen when the doors were opened.

divisionism/optical mixing: a method of dividing colour using the properties of light. Colour was mixed on the *canvas* rather than on the *palette*. The late nineteenth-century scientific theories of colour and light by the American scientist Ogden Rood, and Michel-Eugene Chevreul's laws of simultaneous contrasts, led the French artists Georges Seurat and Paul Signac to apply dots of pure *primary colours* close together to create stronger, clearer versions of the resulting *secondary colours*. Points of colour carefully placed on the canvas come together into recognisable shapes when seen by the viewer at a certain distance; colour is optically, rather than physically, mixed. This gives the familiar 'dot' paintings; for example, Seurat's 'The Bathers' and 'La Grande Jatte', 1884–86. Look at the grass in full sunlight, made up of contrasting *complementary colours* — in this case orange and yellow, with some local colour to make green. Look also at the shadows made from blues and greens, with stray dots of yellow and orange to show dappled sunlight. This interest in optically mixing colour extended to placing complementary colours on the borders of the work to affect the colours next to them in the actual painting. Notice that these pure dots of colour, if mixed at all, were only blended with white, and the dot of paint varied in size according to the scale of the picture and the position of the dot within it. The earlier *Impressionists* had used a similar system of optical mixing, by placing shades and *tones* of a colour next to each other to make them seem more brilliant, or to create the shimmering effect of light — e.g. Claude Monet's 'Autumn Effect at Argenteuil', 1873, Courtauld Institute Gallery, London, which has warm yellows and pinks against small touches of green to create autumnal effects. Impressionist colour theory also claimed that because black did not occur in nature, it should not be used in paintings about nature, so shades of grey were used to create the effect of black.

Known at the time as *Neo-Impressionism*, or *pointillism*, the subject matter of divisionism was, like Impressionism, modern city life and some traditional landscape, although divisionism was considered a progression from Impressionism. Although many artists found the act of making a Neo-Impressionist painting too tedious a formula, the idea of dividing colour and the search for intensity and vibrancy using pure colours endured. Seurat's semi-scientific investigations made the removal of colour from its functional, purely descriptive purpose possible, and allowed subsequent artists to use it in an abstract manner.

■ *When:* 1886–1906, Paris.

■ *Who:* Georges Seurat and Paul Signac.

■ *Links: additive mixing, colour, subtractive mixing.* Looks forward to *Post-Impressionism* and the use of colour by artists like van Gogh and Gauguin; also the extremely bold colouring of the *Fauves*. Seurat's drawings show a continuing interest in light; they use strong contrasts of light and dark to make powerful images — well worth looking at. Look at scientific theories of light from Newton onwards and try investigating the difference between *additive mixtures* and the *Ben Day process*.

■ *Formal elements:* tone, colour, form, pattern, texture.

Divisionists: not to be confused with *divisionism*, the Divisionists were members of an Italian art movement who shared similar technical aims, but who had a clear political motive — to show the appalling conditions of the workers, e.g. Angelo Morbelli's 'For Eighty Cents', 1895, Civico Museo Antonio Borgogna, Vercelli, a painting that represents peasants weeding rice. Although an attractive painting, its subject matter is less than pleasant.

■ *When:* late nineteenth to early twentieth century.

■ *Who:* Angelo Morbelli, Giovanni Segantini, Giussepe Pelliza da Volpedo.

■ *Links:* Divisionism was one of the sources of *Futurism*. Boccioni's early work, e.g. 'The City Rises', 1910, Museum of Modern Art, New York, shows a clear debt to the Divisionists in its combination of colours.

drawing: a picture or plan made by means of *lines* on a surface. It is the fundamental tool for visual research, the first method by which any artist finds out about the world around them, and a method that you have to use to succeed at any level in this subject. In making a drawing, an artist is investigating structure. Drawing involves much more than a small *tonal* study of an object floating on the empty white page of a sketchbook. In drawing we are trying to find out what we can see in front of us, not reproduce what we already know.

The type of drawing will vary according to the subject — a moving figure needs large-scale, quick marks (charcoal is a good medium to work in), echoing the overall shapes. On the other hand, the first visual investigations of a single flower bud might demand a small piece of perfect hand-made paper and the sharpest pencil. Drawing is an analytical process; although the result might be a finished product (a beautiful tonal work for example), this is not the intention of the drawing method. John Ruskin (the nineteenth-century English art critic and champion of Turner, whose architectural drawings and *landscape* sketches are fascinating) said that we draw not in order to produce good drawing, but so that we may learn to see.

■ *Links:* Constable's landscape drawings, many of which are on show at the Victoria and Albert Museum, London, show quick landscape sketches, made with the comparatively new *medium* of lead pencil. They display a variety of individual marks (see *autographic mark*) used to describe the forms of trees and clouds. In other words, by varying the type of pencil mark according to the *organic* qualities of the subject, Constable is developing his own *visual language*. Albrecht Dürer, the greatest figure of the Northern *Renaissance* in the late fifteenth to early sixteenth century, was both a painter and a printer. His knowledge of *woodcut*, engraving and the relatively new medium of *etching* meant that he was especially skilled in the use of line and, unusually for his time, he drew constantly, keeping sketchbooks on his journey from Germany to Italy. Like his contemporaries he drew to make notes for larger works, but unlike them he also made sketches just for enjoyment. The benefits of this sort of drawing can be seen in his graphic work. Rembrandt, the great seventeenth century Dutch painter, etcher and draughtsman, also drew constantly. His drawings, like his paintings, show a fascination with the effects of light and the rendering of tone.

Van Gogh took this process further, e.g. 'Garden at Saint-Remy', 1889, Tate Modern, London. Influenced by the flat colours and contours of Japanese woodcuts, he used pen and ink (which does not have the same opportunities of tonal range as the pencil), so the drawing is made up of a series of clear, short strokes, some straight for grass and a fence, some curving slightly to show types of foliage, others spiralling wildly to show trees in the wind. Cézanne, another key *Post-Impressionist*, pointed out that lines drawn horizontally appear to go away from the eye and create depth, while lines drawn vertically act like a fence and stop the eye. Try cutting your own reed pens, like van Gogh. Take a piece of bamboo and shape the end into a flat quill not unlike the nib of a fountain pen: the wider the nib the broader the stroke; the thinner the nib the more flexible it is. To produce his slow, curving lines echoing the forms of the women he was drawing, Matisse not only stuck his *brushes* onto long canes but also used sticks of charcoal in the same way.

The materials you can use for drawing are endless — Degas' studies in pastels, e.g. 'After the Bath, Woman Drying Herself', 1895, Courtauld Gallery, London, are clearly a form of drawing, in that you can see a series of individual strokes of *colour* as he tries to find the shape of the female body in front of him. Not only that, he has added on many pieces of paper, as he extended the original subject to include new areas of interest. David Hockney made series of drawings using biros. Chalks and charcoal are the classic media, but anything that will make a mark that has some relationship to the subject studied will do. Likewise the support or *ground* you work on does not have to be pure white cartridge paper.

Remember, do not isolate an object. Each thing that you draw has a context, whether it is the physical space around it and the shadows it casts or the 'art space' you put the object into, composed of further visual research on the effect of colour and textural relationships.

■ *Formal elements:* all.

drip painting: another name for the *gestural painting* of *Abstract Expressionist* artists, and in particular the work of Jackson Pollock.

■ *Links: Abstract Expressionism, gestural painting.*

■ *Formal elements:* line, colour, pattern, texture.

Earth art: see *Land art*.

easel/easel painting: the easel is a device for holding a painting at suitable working height in the vertical plane.

Easels can be used for oil painting, where the artist needs the canvas to be at a vertical angle, whereas the watercolourist will need to lay the paper nearly flat, so that the wet paint does not run. To fit onto the easel, paintings need to be of a reasonably small size. The 'death of easel painting' came when artists used canvases of increasing size and changed their methods of applying paint and pigment.

■ *Links: Abstract Expressionism.*

encaustic: see *impasto*.

endorsements: the name given by the exam boards to the specialised areas of art that students may wish to study. Alternatively, they may want to take the broad-based unendorsed course. Currently the endorsements include art and design, fine art, three dimensional design, textiles, photography, graphic design and critical and contextual studies.

engraving: prints made by carving or etching with acid onto a wood block or metal plate. There are two techniques for making engravings — *relief* and *intaglio*. In the *intaglio* printing process, the lines of the design are incised into a sheet of copper or zinc (called the plate) with a tool called a burin, that cuts a V-shaped groove. Ink is rubbed into these lines and the surface of the plate wiped clean with several rags. Paper is laid onto the surface of the plate, several thicknesses of felt blanket are laid on top and these are then put through a powerful copper-plate press. The paper is forced into the lines and picks up the ink that is in them, receiving an impression of the design. Contrast this with *relief* printing, where the parts of the wood block or metal plate which form the design are left in relief and the rest is cut away.

■ *When:* since the fifteenth century.

- *Who:* many artists have used this process, notably Albrecht Dürer in Germany in the sixteenth century and Rubens in the seventeenth.
- *Links:* engraved prints were often the way in which the general public saw paintings; many engravers were employed only in reproducing paintings in print form. For instance, Turner's landscapes were first sold as books of prints.
- *Formal elements:* line and tone.

Environment art: an art form in which the viewer can enter a three-dimensional enclosed space, either inside or outdoors, where all his senses will be stimulated — hearing, smell, touch, and sometimes taste, through the use of lights, sound, colour, etc. Not to be confused with art in the environment, e.g. *Land art*.
- *When:* the 1960s.
- *Links: installation*. Environment art arrived at the same time as *Happenings* and was closely linked with the art of that period.

etching: a method of *intaglio* engraving, in which the design is bitten into the plate with acid. A plate of polished copper is first covered with an acid-resistant material, and the etcher then draws a design on the grounded plate with a steel etching needle. The back and edges of the plate are covered with an acid-resisting varnish called 'stopping-out varnish' and the plate is immersed in a bath of dilute acid, usually nitric, which bites into the metal wherever the plate has been exposed by the needle. It is the biting of the acid that makes etching different from engraving; etchers can vary the depth and amount of the acid's effect and the resulting qualities of the final print are similar to those of line drawings. When the etcher is satisfied with the effects of the acid 'biting', the plate is cleaned and printing is carried out in the same way as for engraving. Unlike relief printing, where the ink is carried on the raised surface of the block, the ink stays in the grooves made by the needle and then the acid. The ink is printed onto the paper through great pressure in a printing press.
- *When:* since the seventeenth century.
- *Links:* etching is important because it allows artists to reproduce a drawn line and is considered a more fluid, less formal medium than engraving. Look, for instance, at Giovanni Piranesi's series of etchings of imaginary prisons, 'I Carceri', begun in 1745. These strange, dark images had a great influence on the later *Surrealists* and probably twentieth-century designers of horror films. Look, also, at Picasso's late engravings. Goya made many series of etchings — the 'Disasters of War' (1810–29) were particularly shocking: 22 images of war at its most brutal.
- *Formal elements:* line.

Expressionism: there are two meanings to the word — the most familiar being the art movement in the first half of the twentieth century that stressed subjective experience.

Expressionism (with a capital 'E') was a movement in architecture, drama, film and literature, as well as painting, about emotion — not about the appearance of things but the feelings they create (see also *Der Blaue Reiter* and *Die Brücke*). In direct contrast to *Impressionism*, for instance, which concentrated on painting the appearance of things, the key word here is subjective. Expressionism owed a great deal to the earlier *Post-Impressionists* (van Gogh and Gauguin especially), in particular the use of bright, non-naturalistic colour in a conscious and emotional exaggeration of nature, applied in thick strokes, without any attempt to reproduce light and modulate areas of tone; a flat application of paint deliberately ignoring three-dimensionality. Gauguin, like the *Cubists*, was fascinated by non-European art, and African masks and wood carvings were important for the Expressionists. The Norwegian artist, Edvard Munch, also used strong colour and distortion to express emotion, and, with Gauguin, revived the technique of woodcutting (see *woodcut*). His exploration of its powerful qualities greatly influenced the German Expressionists. Expressionist art was later reinvented under the title Neue Sachlichkeit (New Objectivity) in the 1920s and early 1930s. Artists like Max Beckman, Otto Dix and George Grosz made art full of bitterness and cynicism about society after the First World War.

The other use of the term expressionism (with a small 'e') refers to the subjective use of line, colour and form, rather than the naturalistic copying of nature. This process can be traced right back through the history of art, and the artist who typifies this style is Mathias Grünewald, and his 'Isenheim Altar', 1510–15, Musée d'Unterlinden, Colmar, France. This great altarpiece shows the tortured Christ on the cross, his skin pierced all over with thorns, his hands writhing against the nails that crucify him.

■ *When:* Expressionism lasted from 1905 to 1930 in Germany, although the *Fauves* in France were also exploring similar uses of paint in 1905.

■ *Who:* the two key groups were *Die Brücke* (Dresden, 1905–13), and *Der Blaue Reiter* (Munich, 1911–14).

■ *Links: Abstract Expressionism* developed in the United States after the end of the Second World War in 1945. Painters such as Mark Rothko, Willem de Kooning, Franz Kline and Jackson Pollock used gestures and pure paint to show emotions without the recognisable subject matter of the earlier Europeans. *Der Blaue Reiter, Die Brücke*; see *Fauvism* and *Post-Impressionism* for the use of colour.

■ *Formal elements:* colour, form, texture.

Fauves/Fauvism: a loose grouping of French artists based around Henri Matisse in the early twentieth century, who took *Impressionist* subject matter, e.g. modern urban life and the newly developing idea that painting could be the formal organisation of colours upon a surface. The Fauves used pure, unbroken colour which was freed from its traditional descriptive role. Matisse's famous painting of his wife, 'Portrait with the Green Stripe', 1905, Copenhagen State Museum, for instance, shows a flattening of the face and a long vertical green stripe running from his wife's hair down her nose to her chin. He ignores representational precision, and uses colour as the subject of the painting. 'What I am after, above all, is expression,' Matisse wrote in 1908.

◼ *When:* 1904–08.

◼ *Who:* Georges Braque, André Derain, Raoul Dufy, Henri Matisse, Maurice de Vlaminck.

◼ *Links:* divisionism, Expressionism, Post-Impressionism. Fauvist colour owed a great deal to van Gogh — compare Matisse's 'Portrait with the Green Stripe' to van Gogh's 'Portrait of the Artist with Severed Ear', 1889, Leigh B. Block Collection, Chicago. Examine carefully the colour in the backgrounds of both paintings, especially the division into strong areas of pure complementary colours and the relationship of those areas to the colours on the face; they are all trying to intensify the effect of colour, which is one of the basic intentions of Fauvism. Georges Braque was a Fauve before he saw Picasso's painting 'Les Demoiselles d'Avignon', which led him to develop *Cubism* with Picasso. Try following Braque's personal progression with work of your own.

Both Braque and Matisse studied Cézanne; Matisse bought Cézanne's painting, 'The Three Bathers', 1905–06, Petit Palace, Paris. What was it they were both looking for? Look also at the use of colour in *Expressionism* after 1906, when Max Pechstein returned to Germany from Paris with news of Fauvist work. Look back to *divisionism, Post-Impressionism*. A big Cézanne exhibition held in Paris the year after his death in 1906 made many of the Fauve artists rethink the direction of their art — should there be more to painting a subject than the use of outline and bright primary colours? Inspired by late Cézanne paintings of Monte Sainte-Victoire, Braque and Derain thought that they needed to include a clearer investigation of form as well. There are possibilities for some good work of your own here; try following the development of Fauvist art from 1905 to 1908, making a parallel between their work and your own studies of landscape. Remember to include an analysis of the artists who influenced them as well.

■ *Formal elements:* colour, form, pattern, texture.

figurative: painting and sculpture based on the naturalistic representation of the external world, i.e. everything from the human figure, to landscapes, still lives, etc. Figurative work is therefore in contrast to *abstract* art.

fine art: art produced for its aesthetic value. Originally the term was used in contrast to the applied or decorative arts (e.g. ceramics, textiles, furniture, jewellery), the manufacture of which depends on physical skill and hard work. In the eighteenth century the fine arts were listed as painting, sculpture, architecture, poetry and music, and this classification has endured.

Fine art is one of the AS/A-level *endorsements*. The exam boards' definition of fine art is that of a process, a way of working, thinking and communicating ideas, rather than a restrictive set of art practices. For instance, fine art can now also include alternative media, e.g. installation, photography, film, video, and television, as well as traditional methods. Essentially, the fine art endorsement calls for investigative work, resulting from personal experience and observation, rather than work made to a set brief (see *design*). Art work will involve students' individual thoughts, feelings, observations, and ideas, and their interaction with the wider world — social issues, for example. Fine Art will also depend to a large degree on studying the work of others and the conventions of making imagery (critical and contextual studies).

foreground: the area of a painting that appears to be at the front of the pictorial space, i.e. nearest the viewer.

■ *Links: background, midground, perspective.*

foreshortening: a type of perspective used for a line, form or object, to make it look as if it is disappearing into the pictorial space, thereby creating the illusion of a third working dimension: depth. (Flat two-dimensional surfaces have two working dimensions: up and across.) In essence, an object should become narrower and smaller as it moves into the pictorial space.

■ *Links:* one of the first examples is the knight in armour lying in the bottom left of Uccello's 'Battle of San Romano', 1450, National Gallery, London. The foreshortened figure is lying on an *orthogonal* pointing towards the *vanishing point*.

form/formalism: the three-dimensional volume of an object, the space that the object occupies, as opposed to its colour, texture, etc. Also called the *formal elements*.

Formalism is the critical concentration on the purely formal aspects of the work such as line, shape and colour, rather than thinking about the work of art in its representational or social context. Formalism is especially relevant to *abstract* art.

■ *Links:* there are various types of visual research to analyse the form of an object; try wrapping the object tightly in paper or cloth, so that many wrinkles show like contours around it. Put the object in a strong raking light — the series of tonal drawings you make can concentrate on the shadows caused by these creases, demonstrating the form by the light on the wrapping. Try the same process, but wrap the object in cling film so that you can see both contours and prominent features; use a series of *washes* of colour to build up knowledge of the form.

To help visualise the space that this object occupies, you could try putting it (unwrapped) under a running tap. Watch how water bounces off some areas, and runs down others. Look at Degas' drawings studying the form of a woman's back, e.g. 'After the Bath', 1895, Courtauld Gallery, London, and use pastels. Notice how the strokes of the pastel in the Degas drawings run with the curves of the form, whereas an artist like Cézanne made the strokes of his brush go across the form of the object. Lucian Freud's later paintings and drawings use the direction of the visible brushstroke to model the form, e.g. 'Benefits supervisor resting', 1994, in which the folds of the enormous quantity of flesh are made clear by the *impasto* brush strokes.

formal elements: also known as the visual elements, the building blocks of making art: *colour, form, line*, pattern, texture, *tone* and shape. In any unit of examined work, a student must be able to show that they understand how these work, how the elements interact with each other, and that they can analyse how other artists have used them.

■ *Links:* see entry under each individual element.

found object: also known as *objet trouvé*, something removed from its original context and employed in *collages* and *assemblages* or exhibited as an object of interest in its own right, with no, or minimal, alteration.

■ *When:* from the first *Cubist* collage, Picasso's 'Still Life with Chair Caning', 1912, Museé Picasso, Paris. The practice of using objects in art continues today.

■ *Who:* Braque and Picasso used non-art objects in Cubist collages, e.g. 'Bottle of Vieux Marc, Glass, Guitar and Newspaper', 1913, Tate Modern, London. Picasso's sculptures also used actual objects, e.g. 'Head of a Bull' (1943), that combines a bicycle saddle and handlebars to suggest the animal. The *objet trouvé* was a key stylistic device for both *Dada*, e.g. Duchamp's *ready-mades*, and *Surrealism*, e.g. the American artist, Robert Rauschenberg, used objects in his *combine paintings*, e.g. 'Canyon' of 1959, Private Collection, New York, that features a stuffed eagle, photographs, paint tubes and a pillow. Many later American and British Pop artists used actual objects. The British *YBAs* use objects constantly, e.g. Damien Hirst's 'The Physical Impossibility of Death in the Mind of Someone Living', 1991, Saatchi Collection, London, is a 4-metre tiger shark suspended in a huge tank of formaldehyde. Hirst called it 'a thing to describe a feeling', which is a reasonable description of the role of the found object in art.

■ *Links: combine paintings, Cubism, Pop art, ready-made, Surrealism, YBAs.*

fresco: a method of wall painting in which pure powdered pigments, mixed in water, are applied to wet plaster, so that when they both dry the surface is almost permanent and susceptible only to damp and earthquakes. Colours in fresco tend to be light and chalky — blending was difficult and artists used hatching to create modulation. Artists had to work very quickly with the wet plaster and corrections were impossible, unless they hacked the plaster off and started again. Look very carefully at Raphael's 'School of Athens', 1509–11, Stanza della Segnatura, Vatican Museum, Rome, and the figure of Michelangelo (as Heraclitus) in the centre foreground. Raphael was painting this fresco at the same time and in the same building as Michelangelo was working on the Sistine ceiling. Raphael was so impressed by the older man's work that he removed a section of the plaster and painted in a portrait of Michelangelo to show his admiration.

■ *When:* known to have been used in ancient Greece, and the usual method of Roman wall decoration — see for example the Villa of the Mysteries at Pompeii. The high-point of fresco was the Italian *Renaissance*, from Giotto's 'Arena Chapel', Padua, 1305–06, and Masacchio's 'Holy Trinity', 1425, Santa Maria Novella, Florence, through to the triumphant high-point of fresco painting by Michelangelo in the Sistine Chapel, Vatican Museum, Rome, 1510–41. The process continued to be used intermittently until the twentieth century; the last major fresco painters were the Mexican muralists José Orozco, Diego Rivera and David Siqueiros, e.g. Rivera's 'The Making of a Fresco, showing the Building of a City', 1931, San Francisco Art Institute.

■ *Links: cartoon, Renaissance.* The importance of frescoes is their possible size, and the freedom that such a scale allows the artist. The actual techniques are probably impractical nowadays, but the breadth and the limited palette are worth thinking about. The making of huge, experimental cartoon drawings, perhaps using charcoal and chalk on lining or wrapping paper, can be very useful.

frottage: see *decalcomania*.

Futurism: *avant-garde* Italian art movement founded by the Italian writer, Filippo Marinetti, before the First World War, with the publication of a manifesto in the Parisian newspaper, *Le Figaro*, in 1909. Futurism was not restricted to painting but involved all the arts, i.e. sculpture, architecture, music, cinema and photography. For example, Antonio Sant'Elia's drawings were proposals for new Futurist cities, e.g. 'Airport and Railway Station with Elevators and Funiculars over Three-levelled Street', 1914, Museé Civici, Como, Italy. The Futurists were anti-museums and *classical* art; their art was based on an excitement about modern technology and the speed of the new motor cars in particular, e.g. Marinetti: 'A screaming automobile that seems to run like a machine gun is more beautiful than the Victory of Samothrace' (a recently discovered classical statue, see *allegory*). Futurist painters were influenced by *Cubist* concepts, particularly the idea that motion could be represented either on a flat canvas or in three-dimensional sculpture. Picasso and Braque were interested in the behaviour of the artist's eye as its gaze travelled around an object. This inspired them to make paintings that merged the subject as seen from several different angles, and the background, into one entity; essentially in a Cubist painting it is artist who moves, and not the object. However, in a Futurist painting it is the objects being painted that move, and that motion is represented by a series of 'snapshots' superimposed on each other. Futurists often used multiple exposure, photographic studies of movement, e.g. Giacomo Balla's 'Dynamism of a Dog on a Leash', 1912, Albright-Knox Art Gallery, Buffalo, which shows the superimposed images of the fast-moving, small dog seen from the static viewpoint of the pedestrian. The Futurists painted subjects taken from urban life and, unlike the dog painting, were often political in nature.

■ *When:* 1909–29.

■ *Who:* Giacomo Balla, Filippo Marinetti, Gino Severini, Carlo Carrà, Umberto Boccioni.

■ *Links: Cubism, Constructivism, Dada.* Futurism was one of the few art groupings concerned with representing movement. Boccioni's sculpture, 'Unique Forms of Continuity in Space', 1913, Tate Modern, London, does not symbolise movement that has been, but actually represents it happening, as the figure strides forcefully forward — 'the construction of the action of the body' (Boccioni); air seems to wrap around the body as though it was in a wind tunnel. If you are working on the subject of movement, the Futurists are worth studying, and also their effect on others. For instance — Marcel Duchamp's 'Nude Descending a Staircase, no. 2', 1912, Philadelphia Museum of Art, displays multiple images of the nude, and owes a great deal to photography.

Genre: with a capital 'G', a way of organising the different subjects for art, much used by the academic *Salon* of the eighteenth and nineteenth centuries. The subjects were arranged into: history painting or the *Grand Manner* (most important), portraiture, landscape, still life, and genre (least important). This system has been resurrected by the Tate Modern, which now divides its displays into landscape, still life, history, and the nude, but the Tate does not make one category more important than the others.

genre painting: with a small 'g', art depicting scenes from daily life. In the academic system (see *Genre*) it was seen as the lowest subject for art, marked by its high degree of lifelike realism and domesticity.

■ *When:* although this is a subject that goes back to Roman *mosaics*, the most well-known versions were probably from the Netherlands (Holland) in the sixteenth century, which specialised both in scenes from peasant life, e.g. Breughel's 'Peasant Wedding', 1568, Kunsthistorisches Museum, Vienna, and the small dramas of ordinary domestic middle-class life, e.g. Pieter de Hooch, 'The Linen Cupboard', 1663, Rijksmuseum, Amsterdam.

■ *Who:* despite its lack of importance, genre painting has been a constant subject, for instance Vermeer's paintings. Although these seventeenth-century Dutch paintings also appear to be genre work, they are small and typically show the insides of houses. Vermeer's art appears to show everyday activities, but the beautiful painting of light and careful use of the new science of optics have always stretched the boundaries of the term. For instance, the 'Art of Painting', 1670, Kunsthistorisches Museum, Vienna, could just be a scene from the artist's life as he worked at home, or it could be a careful *allegory* about the role of painting. Later genre work, e.g. by Jean-Simeon Chardin, continues the theme of the interior and unremarkable life of a household — see the 'Young Schoolmistress', 1740, National Gallery, London, which shows a child teaching a younger one to read in a darkened space, neither one looking out of the canvas at the viewer. Although the majority of the pioneers of the early

g

twentieth century, for instance Cézanne and subsequently the *Cubists*, tended to focus on *still life*, ordinary domestic life has continued to feature as a subject. Rauschenberg's 'Bed', 1955, oil and pencil on pillow, quilt and sheet on wood supports, Museum of Modern Art, New York, could be said to continue the theme (see *combine paintings*). Certainly Tracey Emin's work does, and not only her diary-like prints in which she writes up her thoughts, but also the appliquéd quilts, and most obviously her 'Bed', 1998, Saatchi Collection, London — a presentation of the artist's bed, which, in all its seedy glory, continues the genre approach (see *YBAs*).

■ *Links:* landscape, still life.

gestural painting: a style of painting in which the creation of the painting is clearly recorded in the marks on the canvas, which are the reason for the work. The gestures of the artist, using expressive brushwork on a large scale, reveal the artist's personality, or ideally the artist's inner being, to the viewer. The *Modernist* use of this technique owed a great deal to *automatic writing*.

■ *When:* although the use of obvious brushwork to show the personality of the artist goes back to *Romanticism* and before, gestural painting is usually associated with European *Expressionism* and the later American *Abstract Expressionism*.

■ *Who:* Willem de Kooning, Jackson Pollock, Marc Tobey.

■ *Links: Abstract Expressionism, action painting, automatic writing, Expressionism.*

glaze: a thin, transparent layer of paint applied over another *colour*, so that these layers create depth by means of light being reflected back from the under surface and modified by the glaze. The effect achieved by applying a glaze is quite unlike that of mixing the two pigments together as a *wash* applied to pure white paper (see *watercolour*). Glazes give the illusion of depth and light, which is especially useful in *oil painting* for suggesting drapery and skin. The same process is used in ceramics to create a waterproof covering, and either is a decoration in itself or protects the decoration applied to the clay.

■ *Who:* although van Eyck did not invent oil painting as was once thought, he did work on the use of glazes. His technique was to glaze oils over a **tempera** ground, so that the quick-drying egg **tempera** could be combined with the slower drying, richer colours of layered oil paint. Look, for instance, at his 'Arnolfini Marriage', 1434, National Gallery, London, where the saturated colours of the greens in the lady's clothing and deep shadows in the reds on the bed are produced by layers of glaze on an opaque under-layer. Later artists experimented further, extending the use of oil glazes, for instance Leonardo da Vinci's use of **sfumato**, or the smoky haziness of blended tones made by layers of transparent glazes, e.g. 'Mona Lisa', 1503–06, Musée du Louvre, Paris, the famous smile built up by immensely subtle glazes. The British artist, Turner, in the nineteenth century, used glazing with bravura.

g

The 'Fighting Temeraire', 1838, National Gallery, London, shows a wide combination of all the properties of oil paint: opaque blue and pink body colour in the sky, for example, overlaid by yellow and pink glazes as well as *scumbled* whites, yellows and reds to convey the power of the sun. Turner was known as an experimenter with painting techniques, working with varnishing glazes even as a painting was about to be exhibited. Towards the end of the nineteenth century, and certainly during the early twentieth century, artists stopped using glazes, preferring to paint directly using increasingly pure body colour (e.g. *Fauvism*).

golden section: name given to the proportion made by dividing a line into two unequal sections, so that the ratio of smaller part is to the larger as the larger is to the whole. This is a division made naturally by the eye and is considered especially harmonic. The golden section was studied in ancient Greece by mathematicians and rediscovered during the *Renaissance*.

■ *Links: composition, perspective, Renaissance.*

Gothic: term describing the art of the Middle Ages, lasting from the beginning of the twelfth to the sixteenth centuries in all the arts of Europe. The English Gothic revival in the eighteenth century established it as the alternative style to *classicism*. Since the late eighteenth century the word Gothic has also been used to describe anything that is gloomy, vaguely medieval and slightly sinister.

The key characteristics of Gothic architecture are: pointed or vaulted arches, buttresses and flying buttresses, and elaborate, organically-derived decoration, in contrast to the smooth, plain walls of the later classically-inspired *Renaissance* buildings. The reduction in wall space in the great cathedrals led to the use of stained glass in windows instead of paintings. Compare the high point of English Gothic: Kings College Chapel, Cambridge, 1446–1515 (especially the astonishingly ornate roof where the pointed arches are just visible under the fan vaulted decoration), with the New Sacristy, Medici Chapel by Michelangelo, 1519, Florence. His chapel has plain walls, classical decoration, a simple roof, and a purely symmetrical plan.

It is this use of detail and intensity that also characterises Gothic art — for instance, the 'Wilton *Diptych*', 1395 or later, artist unknown, National Gallery, London. These two small panels, in the late International Gothic style, are full of paintings of flowers, all of which have symbolic meanings, as well as the careful painting of the Virgin, the angels with their huge bird-like wings that create repeated patterns across the back of the panel, and Richard II with his attendant saints. Richard's cloak, for example, is encrusted with small pearls to form images of broom pods, the personal symbol of the Plantagenet family.

■ *When:* starting with the architecture of the twelfth century in France, Gothic was at first almost entirely devoted to Christian cathedral building, but in the thirteenth century was extended to monastic architecture, parish churches and domestic architecture. Gothic ended its domination of Europe in about the sixteenth century.

■ *Links: Classical*, the *Renaissance*. In Italy, Giotto set new standards in the transition between Gothic and the Early Renaissance, e.g. the Arena Chapel, 1305–06, Padua. In this chapel Giotto painted frescoes that begin to introduce the illusion of the physical weight of the painted figures; they appear as individual beings occupying space — one of the key characteristics of the High Renaissance.

■ *Formal elements:* colour. The high point of Gothic art in terms of colour is the stained glass at Chartres Cathedral in France, especially the use of red and blue, the colours of the passion of Christ and of the Virgin Mary.

Pattern: look at the use of repeated pattern, particularly in architecture, e.g. on the West Portal (door) of Chartres Cathedral, 1145–70. The figures are standing in carved columns, their drapery making either vertical folds in regular repeats, or diagonal folds — both methods entirely unlifelike. The figures stand on columns that are further decorated with geometric patterns of squares or interwoven lines and areas. Compare this use of pattern with the figures on the North Portal of Chartres, 1194, where the sculptors have started to look at both classical sculpture and possibly how cloth actually folds; certainly the figures are more life-like. So what is the role of pattern in the sculpture on these two doors?

gouache: a water-based paint that is opaque when dry, as opposed to the transparent *washes* used in *watercolour*, for instance. The finished surface of gouache paint is dense and quite dry; the paint appears to be more thickly applied than it actually is and, unlike acrylic paint, it has no polymer binders and therefore no shine. Gouache tends to be sold in small tubes with unfamiliar names for the pigments. Although expensive, these tubes are often sold in discount sales and are very useful as an extra medium to use with acrylics and watercolour. Also, because gouache does not flow heavily and is easily controlled in small areas with an intense colour, it is a good medium to use for graphic work.

Grand Manner: the name given by the French academies to the style used for history painting in particular, based on the methods of Raphael, Poussin and the Carracci brothers. The essential aim of the Grand Manner was to make art better than ordinary nature, so the little details of, for instance, landscape or portraiture were left out in favour of either figures wearing imitation classical drapery, or ideal nudes with stressed muscles and lots of dramatic gestures.

■ *When:* from the *Renaissance* until the end of the nineteenth century. The term was first used in the seventeenth century.

g

■ *Who:* any artist who wanted to make their name — for example, Nicholas Poussin's 'The Abduction of the Sabine Women', 1636–37, Metropolitan Museum of Art, New York. Compare the extraordinary display of emotion (figures frozen like statues, many references to the classical past, lots of ***contrapposto***, etc.) with the art that deliberately tried to replace the Grand Manner, e.g. *realism*, and Gustave Courbet's 'Bonjour Monsieur Courbet', 1854, Musée Fabre, Montpellier. Although equally large, Courbet's painting shows the artist meeting his patron (the man who supports him by buying his art). It is an ordinary subject, nature is accurately portrayed, the gestures are no longer heroic, thus heralding the death of the Grand Manner.

■ *Links: Genre, history painting, Neo-classicism, realism.*

graphic art: the overall term for drawings and print-based works on paper (e.g. etching, woodcut engraving).

ground: the surface on which the art work is made, paper for *watercolour* or *acrylic* paintings, *canvas* perhaps for oil painting or acrylic, or maybe a wooden board (thin-ply, MDF, hardboard, etc.) suitably primed, usually with white emulsion paint. Experimenting with different grounds can bring excellent results; for instance, does the ground need to be brilliant white? Traditionally painters used a brownish colour to give the mid-tones of their work, and in the first sketches just added the highlights and the darker tones to start building up the image. Nor does the ground have to be entirely flat; paper has a 'tooth' to it, that is, the small fibres that make up the material. The stronger the tooth (the rougher the paper), the more the fibres can catch the brush and its contents, or the pencil dragged over it. If you are using a wooden support or ground, you can stretch material over it to make the surface more absorbent, for example many students stretch cheap butter muslin over their boards to give a canvas-like effect. You could take this process further by shaping the muslin to follow the work you are going to do on top of it, perhaps even making a raised ground in suitable areas.

Happening: an art form and form of entertainment, in which the artwork was an action, an assemblage of events that involved the viewer in one way or another. This action was improvised, spontaneous and provocative, impossible to reproduce and usually kept as a video or film that used the grainy, wobbly camera look to support authenticity.

■ *When:* from the 1960s, starting in America.

■ *Who:* Allan Kaprow, Jim Dine, Claes Oldenburg, Robert Rauschenberg, the Fluxus group.

■ *Links: Dada*. Also shares characteristics with *Performance art*, but Happenings had little planning or choreography. Early Claes Oldenburg work featured Happenings; look also at the Fluxus group of artists, for instance Yoko Ono's 'Cut Piece', 1964, in which members of the audience each cut off a piece of her clothing until nothing was left.

Hard-Edge Painting: abstract painting featuring cleanly defined, often geometrical, areas of colour — in other words very different from the expansive brush strokes in *gestural painting* of the earlier *Abstract Expressionists*. It was a similar movement to that of *Colour Field Painting*, that treated the picture plane as a single flat area with no difference between figure and ground.

■ *When:* the 1960s and 1970s, largely in America.

■ *Who:* Kenneth Noland, Ellsworth Kelly.

■ *Links: Colour Field Painting*. The machine-made look of some of these paintings points towards *Minimalism*. Many of Ellsworth Kelly's seemingly abstract paintings, e.g. 'White Curve', 1974, Tate Modern, London, are taken from fragments of everyday life, objects and part of the landscape. The curve in this case is a geometrically accurate segment of a circle and refers to hills and valleys near his home in Chatham, New York. The same process would be worth following — from a series of drawings, choose a section that can be reduced and hugely enlarged in a minimal palette.

historicism: a revival, and an obsession with repeating exactly earlier artistic styles, in order to make a new style, e.g. *Neo-classicism*.

history painting: the illustration of historical events, or mythological, Biblical and literary themes, which were either realistic or idealised. History painting was considered the highest art form by the French academies, characterised by the huge size of the works made, the *Grand Manner* in which they were painted and the complex references to the past. This still happens today, when the biggest works are often considered the most important. History painting was followed in the hierarchy by portraiture, landscape and still life, with *Genre* considered to be inferior.

■ *When:* from the *Renaissance* until the end of the nineteenth century.

■ *Who:* any artist who wanted to make their name.

■ *Links: Genre, Grand Manner.*

hue: what we really mean by *colour*, the dominant wavelength of light that corresponds to a named colour, i.e. the part that produces the colourness of a colour, the redness of red, although the other attribution of colour is *saturation*.

icon: an image of a saint or other suitably holy person, especially in the Byzantine Church, and Greek and Russian Orthodox Churches. They were believed to act as channels between the worshipper and the sacred person to whom the prayers were directed. Icons were first painted onto panels, rather than frescoes, and were therefore relatively small. The rules for making these icons were very strict, following rigid patterns and strict traditions that had survived from *classical* art. The features and characteristics of the holy images did not change; they became stylised and repetitious, but they were the only real survivors of classical art and were important for the early *Renaissance*. Compare the 'Madonna Nikopoeia' icon, from the twelfth century, San Marco, Venice, with Duccio's *triptych* of 'Virgin and Child with St Dominic and St Aurea', 1310–20, National Gallery, London. The Virgin is facing the front in the icon, although side-on in the altarpiece, but the essential features of her face are the same in both, as are the stylised hands. Duccio's painting shows the beginnings of the *naturalism* that characterises the Renaissance, as art starts to build on the Byzantine approach to representing form that we can see in the surviving icons and larger mosaics.

Recently the meaning of the word icon has extended to mean a typical or classic example, and of course it is the name given to the small pictures on a computer desktop, that link you to various functions when you click on them.

■ *When:* one of the first known icons was of St John the Evangelist in about 200 AD. The high point of Byzantine art was lost with the Crusades and the sacking of Constantinople in 1204. The cult of icons spread to Russia from Greece and they are still part of Greek and Russian Orthodox Christian worship today.

■ *Links:* in the sense that an icon means a particular well-known person or example, Andy Warhol's silk-screened images of the famous took the modern approach to iconography, e.g. 'Gold Marilyn Monroe', 1962, Museum of Modern Art, New York. Repeating her graphically reduced face in the centre of a gold background presents just the key elements of the icon that we have come to know as Marilyn Monroe, and also reveals the empty nature of her celebrity; a process emphasised by 'Marilyn Monroe's Lips', 1962, Smithsonian Institution, Washington DC — a *diptych* containing 168 nearly identical silk-screened versions of her lips. In the same way that the identity of any tenth-century saint would be recognised by the attributes painted next to the idealised figure (St Jerome always has a lion, John the Baptist always has an animal skin), Warhol realised that the famous also need these visual attributes in order to be recognisable. This process still exists — it would be an interesting project to take various twenty-first century figures and reduce them to their attributes in the same manner. But remember that Warhol's work also took in the contemporary methods of mass production of imagery: how are images designed and made today? What are the visual characteristics of this new language of image making? Can you identify and reuse those characteristics as part of the art you will be making? Is it possible to combine the two more recent meanings for the term icon? Just photocopying and pasting Jennifer Lopez's attributes into your work journal is not going to get you very far, without placing that image into the context of some serious visual research.

iconoclasm: the destruction of images, a process that started in the early Christian church in the eighth century. Until the Reformation in the sixteenth century, English churches and cathedrals were a riot of colour and paintings, but the rise of the Protestant Church under Henry VIII and the subsequent iconoclasm has led to the white spaces you see now. An iconoclast can mean a destroyer of religious images; its more modern meaning is someone who attacks all the beliefs that a society holds to be most important. In this sense, many 'modern' artists have been iconoclasts.

iconography/iconology: the study of the subject matter of a work of art, an approach to art history that identifies, describes, classifies and interprets the subject matter of the visual arts. Broadly speaking, this means that iconography deals with exactly what you can see in a painting, print, sculpture etc. — who the people are for example, what the symbols mean, how other artists have used them in the past and so on.

Iconology is usually used to mean all of the above, plus the wider study of how different societies have understood art and art history in different eras. This depends on the idea that the visual arts are not self-contained; they are part of a larger culture which is heavily influenced by social and economic conditions. In practice the distinction between iconography and iconology is vague and, increasingly, they mean roughly the same thing.

iconostasis: a screen in Byzantine and Russian Orthodox churches that divides the sanctuary (the priest's part) from the main body of the church (where the laity may go). This screen was covered with *icons*.

ideal: term meaning art which shows the best of nature, and improves upon it. It also referred to the *Renaissance* interest in *Classical* thought and Plato's doctrine that it was the artist's task to show the eternal truths, the ideal perfection behind ordinary nature, rather than reproducing the mundane. This was important because it meant that artists could show they were more than mere copyists, they were in fact philosophers and scientists, worth greater social respect than other craftsmen (and, of course, more money). In contrast to this were those artists who used the developed Renaissance style to show actual life, e.g. Caravaggio (see *Baroque*), Courbet (see *realism*), who were heavily criticised because they were making work that attacked the fundamental rules which guaranteed the importance of art in the first place.

■ *When:* from the *Renaissance* until the end of the nineteenth century.

■ *Who:* any artist who wanted to make their name.

■ *Links: Baroque, Classical, realism.* The representation of the ideal underpins *history painting* and the *Grand Manner*. The search for the ideal could also be described as part of the Utopian art of movements like *De Stijl*, although the pure abstraction they sought was fundamentally opposed to the nude figures and grand gestures that characterised those earlier forms of the ideal. Since the early 1930s, the use of ideal figures and surroundings as propaganda in *Socialist Realism* and *Nazi art* has tainted this type of work.

illusion/illusionism: painting which, with *foreshortening, linear perspective* and painterly devices such as blended modulation of colour and *aerial perspective,* creates the optical appearance of three dimensions and deep space on a two-dimensional surface. Also known as *verisimilitude* or looking like the real thing. The question to ask is: why should artists want to use such a skill, and why should viewers find it so special? What is it, for example, about that type of illusionism, the ***trompe l'oeil*** effect (in which the eye is briefly tricked into thinking a painted object or space is in fact real), that audiences find appealing?

■ *When:* illusion has been part of the appreciation of art since Greek times. The fifth century BC artist Zeuxis apparently painted a bunch of grapes with such illusionistic skill that birds tried to pick at the painting. His rival, Parrhasius, then painted a ***trompe l'oeil*** curtain over the grapes so convincingly that Zeuxis himself tried to pull it away. This story was often repeated to encourage painters to work towards the perfect illusionism of these *Classical* artists. Since *Modernism* few artists have practised such skills, preferring more honest forms of representation.

■ *Links: Classical, ideal, oil paint,* **Vanitas** (illusionistic paintings usually depend on the qualities of this medium and its ability to mimic the depth of skin tone and the tactile nature of materials). If you see paintings which include grapes or curtains, you know that the artist is making reference to the original myth, e.g. Adriaen van der Spelt and Frans van Mieris's 'Still Life with a Flower Garland and a Curtain', 1658, Art Institute of Chicago, which shows a blue silk curtain pulled over a quarter of the painting of flowers and fruit.

■ *Formal elements:* colour, form, tone.

impasto: thick, opaque (not transparent) paint applied with a palette knife, spatula or brush, in which the brush strokes can still be seen and the paint itself can often create a three-dimensional effect. Paint that sticks above the picture surface will catch the light and draw attention to itself as a material, rather than being an invisible part of an *illusion*.

■ *Links:* you can easily make heavy impasto with oil paint by not using any medium to thin the paint (see *oil paint*). Acrylics will need either a specialist gel medium or a modelling paste mixed in with them, or something cheaper and quicker to find, such as sand, wallpaper paste or PVA. Watercolour, based on a series of stains or *washes*, is unsuitable. Although *gouache* paint is thick, the uniform nature of the colour means that the thickness of the surface is sometimes difficult to detect. If you have access to a machine for melting wax, e.g. those used for batik, any pigment can be dissolved in wax and then applied to a board or canvas (a textured surface is best). You can achieve very heavy impasto with wax — the method is called *encaustic* and was first used by the ancient Greeks.

Impressionism: an art movement involving a group of French painters in the late nineteenth century. The movement was anti-academic in that the subject matter of their paintings was not based on traditional themes (see *Grand Manner*) and their work was exhibited in places other than the official *Salon*. The key points of Impressionism are:

- The artists attempted to paint the optical effects surrounding the outside of an object or scene, without *narrative* or, in theory, the intervention of the artist in any way. As Cézanne said of Monet, 'he was just an eye, but what an eye'. Impressionism was about the artist's eye and its interaction with the landscape via paint, paintings about the entire visual field of the whole canvas rather than the individual details and separate forms within it (see *composition*).

- Up to this time, art depended on underpainting, drawing and the role of the line. Line puts an edge around an object; it interprets the object and explains it to the viewer. Impressionists worked directly with paint (see ***plein air painting***), recording their impressions of the entire scene without interpretation, choosing subjects in which the linear approach was impossible, for example water, steam and fog. Monet talked about the 'envelope' between the subject and himself, like the London fog, which he painted in a series from 1870 on: 'For me a landscape does not exist in its own right, since its appearance changes at every moment; but the surrounding atmosphere brings it to life, the air and the light, which vary continually. For me, it is only the surrounding atmosphere that gives subjects their true value'.

- Impressionists chose subjects that were modern, taking the contemporary French writer, Baudelaire's, definition of modernity as 'the fleeting, the transitory, the contingent' (see *modern* and *Modernism*). So Manet and Renoir painted, for example, a fashionable café, e.g. Monet's 'Bathers at La Grenouillere', 1869, and Renoir's 'La Grenouillere', 1869, Nationalmuseum, Stockholm, working side by side.

- Impressionists worked outside in the open air (***plein air***). This meant that the canvases were small so that they could be carried to the subject. In the late eighteenth and early nineteenth centuries advances in chemistry had produced many new manufactured pigments, e.g. zinc white, cobalt blue and, most importantly, an artificial ultramarine to replace the very expensive mineral lapis lazuli (see *colour*). These bright new colours were sold already prepared, so that artists no longer needed to grind their own colours. But it was the invention in 1841 of the collapsible metal paint tube that had profound implications for painting. Artists could now take a range of ready-made paints with them to the scene they wanted to paint. These paints were thicker than those previously used in the studio, so that artists' suppliers also started selling a wide variety of thicker brushes and palette knives to cope with this new paint texture — you can see the effect of those new materials and tools in subsequent Impressionist paintings. The conventions governing art had always demanded that important paintings were large (see *history painting*).

- The Impressionists' method of painting changed the subsequent history of art. If you investigate the way Monet creates form in, for instance, 'Autumn Effect at Argenteuil', 1873, Courtauld Institute Gallery, London, you will see the different methods used. There is no ***chiaroscuro*** modelling, no gradation from light to dark, as in, for example, a painting by Caravaggio.

The characteristic broken brushwork of classic Impressionism comes from the speed of the brush stroke as it tries to record changing light conditions. Form in Monet's 'Autumn Effect at Argenteuil' is created by colour, particularly the contrast between orange and blue. Look at the trees on the right-hand side, where depth is indicated by smudges of blue on top of the orange. Recession, or the *illusion* of depth, is also created both by the diminishing size of brush strokes, which are large closest to the eye and smallest at the horizon, and by the horizontal line of deeper blue across the centre of the painting. There is a series of different types of brush stroke, from the flat horizontal strokes in the foreground which create stability in the composition, to brush-strokes which echo the direction of the leaves in the trees, and even visible scrapings with the brush handle on the right-hand tree indicating bare branches. In other words, the marks of the artist are made evident — a

Essential Word Dictionary

progression from van Gogh's use of *impasto* brush strokes to the arrival of the *autographic mark*, the key feature of painting from now on. Impressionism also made clear the separation of pure colour applied to the canvas from the objects to which the colours were supposed to refer, paving the way for the experiments of artists like Seurat (see *divisionism*) and the *Post-Impressionists*.

■ *When:* term used in 1874 about the first Impressionist exhibition. Impressionism is generally said to have run from 1860 to 1900; its major period of importance was 1869–86.

■ *Who:* Paul Cézanne, Edgar Degas, Édouard Manet, Claude Monet, Camille Pissarro, Pierre-Auguste Renoir, Alfred Sisley and one of the few female artists who belonged to a movement, Berthe Morrisot.

■ *Links:* Abstract Expressionism, divisionism, Modernism, Post-Impressionism, realism.

In Monet's paintings of landscapes and his series of studies of urban life, he tried to paint what he called pure optical reality — just the visual effects. Is this possible? Can painting capture light? Did the Impressionists succeed in this aim and what was the crisis of Impressionism? A good project would be to research this question, following the progress of Monet from the 1860s to the late paintings of water lilies in his garden at Giverny, France.

The Impressionists were only interested in optical realism, not social realism. Most contemporary art now takes the examination of the politics of any subject as part of art. Which approach is right? Why? Try comparing any of Monet's 'Gare St Lazare' series of 1877 with J. M. W. Turner's 'Rain, Steam and Speed' 1844, National Gallery, London. Monet chose to show locomotives resting inside or outside a station rather than rushing through the countryside. The difference between the two artists shows how Impressionism was more realistic, more dispassionate; it had none of Turner's search for the picturesque. As Monet said when he had seen Turner's paintings in London in 1870, Turner was 'antipathetic to him, because of the exuberant romanticism of his fancy'. In other words, Turner chose the right type of subject but Monet would have had to strip away the over-picturesque approach.

installation: *site-specific* artwork created for a particular gallery or space, in which the entire collection or arrangement has to be seen as a whole, not just the discrete hanging of a few particular artworks. Each part of the whole matters and the viewer is surrounded by and immersed in art; not unlike going into a *Gothic* cathedral such as Chartres, although the intention here is not usually to get you to believe in God more fervently!

■ *When:* like *Performance art*, Installation art began in the 1970s, but it can be traced from the 1960s back through the various developments in *Modernism*.

■ *Who:* Barbara Bloom, Damien Hirst, Ed Kienholz, Claes Oldenburg, Richard Wilson.

■ **Links:** the *Surrealist* exhibitions from 1925 onwards, for example, were always more installation than traditional exhibition. Ed Kienholz later made curious tableaux in America, e.g. 'Barney's Beanery', or Claes Oldenburg's 'Store works' from the 1960s. Damien Hirst's 'In and Out of Love', 1991, contains many of the themes and the methods that characterise Hirst's later, more famous, work; the combination of beauty and death, the ways in which we negotiate the only certain fact — death — as identified by Existentialism in the 1950s. What is it to be human, to live, but to have to face death?

intaglio: the metal plate printing processes of engraving or etching, in which the plate is cut away or indented, ink is smeared over the surface, which is then wiped clean and the ink in the recessed areas transfers to the paper. Compare this method with *relief*, where the ink is held on the raised surface before transferring to the paper.

■ **Links:** *engraving, etching, relief, woodcut.*

Jugendstil: the name for the German style of *Art Nouveau*.

Junk art: an art form based on the increasing amount of rubbish produced by Western societies, particularly after the Second World War. The term Junk art refers to a particular type of *assemblage* that used discarded metal, from cars to scrap, to make abstract sculpture, e.g. Richard Stankiewicz' 'Diving to the Bottom of the Ocean', 1958, Musée National d'Art Moderne, Centre Georges Pompidou, Paris, which is a strange collection of machinery parts that create a definite sense of downward movement towards a series of stainless steel tubes; the diver is suggested rather than actual. To an extent these works are a comment on the throwaway society which discarded the metal out of which they are made, but largely they appear to be experiments in three-dimensional *abstraction.*

■ *When:* mostly from the 1950s, although this is a theme that can be traced back to *Cubism* and *collage* via the German *Dadaist* Kurt Schwitters' *Merz* work and the *Surrealist* use of the *found object.*

■ *Who:* Arman, CESAR, Eduardo Paolozzi, Richard S. Stankiewicz, Robert Rauschenberg, Jean Tinguely.

■ *Links:* C*ombine painting, Dada, Pop art.* Look also at the more recent sculptures of the British artist Bill Woodrow — for example his 'Elephant', 1984, Tate Modern, London. The elephant's head is made out of an ironing board and vacuum cleaner mounted like a stuffed colonial trophy on the wall. Its ears are old maps of Africa and South America. In its trunk is a sub-machine gun and beneath it lies a ring of car doors. Unlike earlier Junk art, 'Elephant' is a work that tells a series of stories about the behaviour of European countries towards Africa and South America, a political approach that is common to later *installation.*

■ *Formal elements:* form, pattern, texture.

Kinetic art: art with moving parts, ranging from the simpler types of Kinetic art that move in the air — for example, the mobiles of artists like Alexander Calder dating from the 1940s onwards, through to the fully moving, automated, machine-driven art of, for example, Jean Tinguely, whose 'meta matics' were huge, pointless and noisy machines — see his 'Homage to New York', 1960, a self-destructing installation that took place in the garden of the Museum of Modern Art, New York.

■ *When:* from 1920s to 1970s.

■ *Who:* Alexander Calder, Marcel Duchamp, Naum Gabo, Jean Tinguely.

■ *Links: Op art* paintings often appear to flicker; the *Futurists* proposed moving sculpture, and their static work celebrated movement. Naum Gabo, e.g. 'Standing Wave', 1920, Tate Modern, London, was an early Kinetic artist, but he gave up making art with moving parts because he decided that actual motion was too distracting; it was better to create the movement in the eye of the viewer. His later sculptures with taut wires strung between curved shapes, e.g. 'Linear Construction No. 2', 1949, Private Collection, were hugely influential for a while. Gabo's work brings together *Constructivism* and *organic* form in ways that could still be investigated.

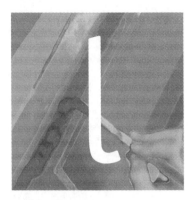

Lamentation: see *Pietà*.

Land art/Earth art: art that uses natural materials such as earth, leaves, water. Land art developed out of *Conceptual art*, and in particular artists wanted to make something that could not be shown in a gallery, as they rejected elitist, fine art traditions and the commercialised world of art galleries. They were much influenced by the ecological movement and back-to-nature hippy ideas of the late 1960s.

Earth art tends to refer to the much larger works created in America — for example, Robert Smithson's 'Spiral Jetty' of 1970, when he made a 457 metre long, 4.6 metre wide spiral out of rock and salt crystals on the edge of the Great Salt Lake, Utah. No one could visit the spiral, nor does it exist any longer. All that remain are the photographs the artist took and a film he made.

Land art tends to describe British art, in particular Richard Long and Andy Goldsworthy — see, for instance, Long's 'Slate Circle', 1979, Tate Britain, London, where rectangular strips of grey slate are arranged in a perfect circle drawn directly onto the gallery floor. Many of Long's sculptures are of natural objects collected during the walks that he takes as part of his art. Although these walks are often recorded with photography and short written pieces, it is the walk that is the art, not the photographs that you see in the gallery.

■ *When:* late 1960s on.
■ *Who:* in the USA, Walter de Maria, James Turrell, Robert Smithson; in the UK, Richard Long, Andy Goldsworthy.
■ *Links: Conceptual art, landscape.*
■ *Formal elements:* pattern, form.

landscape: a painter's term originating in the Netherlands in the sixteenth century. Landscape as a subject for art can be traced back to ancient Egypt. In *Renaissance* art, landscape provided the background to a painting, only occasionally forming part of the subject, e.g. the Garden of Eden. Probably one of the first landscape paintings, in that the figures are set in a realistic landscape, is Giorgione's 'The Tempest', 1505–10, Galleria dell'Accademia, Venice. From the end of the sixteenth century, landscape became a pictorial *genre* in its own right. It was not until the arrival of ***plein air*** *painting* in the nineteenth century that artists started to work outside, rather than recreating the image in their studio from sketches (Gainsborough, the English artist, used broccoli and lumps of coal as inspiration for landscapes). Nowadays, landscapes do not need to be poetic depictions of scenery but can be townscapes, seascapes, maps or abstract images inspired by the experience of landscape.

■ *Links: Genre, Land art, picturesque.* Compare the approach of John Constable, e.g. 'Salisbury Cathedral', 1810, National Gallery, London (his drawings at the Victoria and Albert Museum, London, of the landscape around Hampstead are unusual for the period and show a great interest in actual landscape) with Howard Hodgkin's 'Rain', 1985–89, Tate Britain, London. Both are responses to a place, but as the British artist John Hoyland says: 'They [paintings] are an equivalent to nature, not an illustration of it'.

line: a narrow, continuous mark made by a pencil, pen or paintbrush. One of the *formal elements*. Reducing the world of *tone* and *colour* to a series of lines (linear drawing) through observation demands choice and thought. It is for this reason that line drawing is considered the most superior form of drawing. Paul Klee described drawing as 'taking a line for a walk', and William Blake, the English artist, poet and printer, called it the 'wiry line of truth'. The English painter, William Hogarth, put a 'line of beauty and grace' onto a palette in front of him in his self-portrait, celebrating its importance in the making of art — 'Portrait, the Painter and his Pug', 1745, Tate Britain, London.

There is more to line drawing than simply tracing an outline. For instance, a series of closely-placed lines describes tone; the angle of the line on the page investigates form. Look at van Gogh's drawing of 'Joseph Roulin', 1888, John Paul Getty Museum, Los Angeles, California, made with a reed pen (see *drawing*). The structure of the cheekbones and nose are made by curving groups of cross-hatched lines. Compare this treatment of skin with the hairy mass of the beard and the different length and type of lines.

A drawn line reflects the speed at which it was drawn; this shows in the texture of the mark, the thickness and intensity of the line. The qualities of the subject should determine the speed of the line that analyses it. A large smooth object, landscape, or figure could be responded to with quick, softly drawn strokes, or perhaps the method of drawing a continuous line without stopping or lifting the pencil from the page. A small, spiky object will need short, sharp marks from a very sharp, hard pencil.

The following drawing exercise might help: take a piece of silver foil, crush it slightly, and then take a sharp, hard pencil and draw as much of the foil as you can in half an hour, but only using lines of less than a centimetre long.

Such an exercise forces the eye to concentrate, strengthens the hand-to-eye coordination and shows the effect of using pure line.

■ *Links:* all the other formal elements, *drawing*.

linear perspective: see *perspective*.

linocut: a design cut in relief on lino. It is the form of relief printing most people are familiar with. Linoleum can be expensive to use on any scale, but is relatively easy to cut (warm over a radiator, or with an iron, to make it easier). See *woodcut* for further details.

local colour: the actual or 'true' colour of an object, or area, seen under natural daylight before that colour is affected by reflected light, overshadowing, distance from the eye, etc.

■ *Links: tonal colour*.

Mannerism: has two meanings: it is either the name given to the formal development of the High *Renaissance* in the sixteenth century, or it is the overstatement of expression, and any exaggerated, distorting, surreal or artificial effect.

Mannerism with a capital 'M' is a highly stylised attempt to make a sophisticated emotional impact by depicting stretched and unbalanced figures in distorted pictorial spaces, painted in bright colours. It is a movement that sits between the High Renaissance and the later *Baroque*. Mannerist artists moved away from High Renaissance composition, which insisted on harmony and balance within a painting. For a Mannerist example see Bronzino's 'Venus, Cupid, Folly and Time', 1544–45, National Gallery, London. The central figure is bent back against herself, behind her the elongated figure of a boy kneels on a cushion, clasping her head and chest. Time holds a curtain as a background for the action, and other figures hold strange theatrical poses, extreme versions of classical **contrapposto**. The complexity of this allegory matches the interweaving of the figures, a characteristic of Mannerist art. Compare this to Leonardo's 'Virgin on the Rocks', 1506, National Gallery, London — a calm, solid triangular composition in carefully toned colours.

In the broader sense, the term mannerism, or mannered, can also mean art of any period that is highly stylised, and just recycles old methods, or is excessive in distortion and colour, e.g. late Picasso or Oscar Kokoschka's 'Time Gentleman, Please', 1971–72, Tate Modern, London.

■ *When:* 1510–1600, Italy and France.

■ *Who:* Agnolo Bronzino, El Greco, Giambologna, Jacopo Pontormo, Jacopo Tintoretto, Parmigianino.

■ *Links: Renaissance* — Michelangelo is the obvious link — note the change in his work in the Sistine Chapel, Rome, from the ceiling (1508–12) to 'The Last Judgement' (1536–41) on the wall behind the altar; this later work has Mannerist characteristics. *Expressionism.*

■ *Formal elements:* tone, colour, form.

maquette: a small three-dimensional sketch or model made of clay, wax, mod roc (plaster-impregnated bandage), or whatever is available, made by a sculptor. If you are working in three dimensions, or making **maquettes** to understand how to compose a two-dimensional surface, keep either the objects themselves, or at least a record of them, as a way of showing the progression of your ideas (see *work journal*).

■ *Links: sculpture, work journal.*

media/medium: there are two meanings: the materials that an artist works with, e.g. paint, charcoal, clay, and the techniques and methods for each material; thus painting is one form of medium, *drawing* another, *sculpture* a third and so on. Medium is the singular, media the plural. Medium can also refer to the material that is mixed with pigment to make paint: water for *acrylic* and *watercolour*, turpentine and linseed oil for *oil paints*.

■ *Links:* mixed media describes art works made using more than one material, e.g. *assemblage, installation.*

memento mori: a memento or souvenir is an object that reminds one of past events, so a **memento mori** is a reminder of death. Common symbols are the skull in a **Vanitas** painting or a snuffed-out candle. The recent work of Damien Hirst constantly refers to death in this way (see *YBAs*).

■ *Links: anamorphosis, genre, still life.*

Merz: the name for the collages of the *Dadaist*, Kurt Schwitters, made from everyday objects such as bus tickets, receipts and paper bags. Schwitters also developed a Merz house, or 'Cathedral of Erotic Misery', in Hanover, 1923, (destroyed by allied bombing in 1943 and now reconstructed in the Sprengle Museum, Hanover), a three-dimensional collage or environment made from rubbish. Unlike the earlier *Synthetic Cubist* collages, Merz did not refer to other objects in an illusionistic way; they were complete *abstract* works in themselves. From 1945–48 Schwitters lived in Ambleside, in the Lake District, where he worked on another environment, a Merzbau, in an abandoned barn — this work is now in the Hatton Gallery, Newcastle upon Tyne. It is interesting to speculate what the inhabitants of the Lake District would have made of this leading member of the European *avant-garde* making a Cathedral of Erotic Misery on a wet hillside.

■ *When:* from 1919 to his death in 1948.

■ *Links: collage, Dada, found object, installation.* Many of the YBAs — Damien Hirst in particular — praise Schwitters. Are there any obvious links?

■ *Formal elements:* pattern, texture.

metamorphosis: a complete change from one form to another (in art and literature, especially if it involves magic or the gods).

m

■ *Links:* the *theme* of metamorphosis is a common one, both in the history of art and as an exam topic or starting point. Originally *Metamorphoses* was the title of a collection of mythologies by the classical Roman writer Ovid, which became a great source of stories for later painters, e.g. Antonio and Piero Pollaiuolo's 'Apollo and Daphne', 1470s, National Gallery, London, in which the god Apollo tries to rape the nymph Daphne, but she is saved by her father who turns her into a laurel tree. The painting shows her half way through the transformation, when her arms have become branches but the rest of her body is still female.

The process of change from one state to another is a fertile area for your art. There are straightforward changes like young to old (try looking at Rembrandt's series of self-portraits tracing his progress from youth to old age) or the change from one emotional state to another, but bear in mind that any work must at first be observation-based. You can also use symbol or myth (as above); even the straightforward process of making a piece of art from a series of drawings is an important metamorphosis in itself. The transformation of materials, from thread to textile, from earth to ceramics, are types of meta-morphosis, although materials-based work must be made with studies of the context, intentions and ideas of others to make sure you cover all the assessment criteria.

■ *Formal elements:* all.

midground: the area between the *foreground* and the *background* in a painting.
■ *Links:* foreground, background, *perspective*. Early *Renaissance* painters found the passage between foreground and background difficult, so often the smooth transition through the midground is blocked, e.g. Piero della Francesca arranges the figures in his 'Baptism of Christ', 1445, National Gallery, London, so that the midground is difficult to see.

Minimalism: *abstract* art which has reduced the content and form of the art work to a simple, formal vocabulary, mostly three-dimensional, summed up by the phrase: 'less is more'. A characteristic example is Donald Judd's 'Untitled', 1980, Tate Modern, London, a stack of ten galvanised steel rectangles with blue Perspex inserts mounted vertically like a ladder on the wall. One important principle is the repetition of the generally geometric structures, another is the industrial look and well-made, but impersonal, appearance. Minimalist art excludes all kinds of illusion, metaphor or *narrative* device: 'what you see is what you see', as the minimalist artist Robert Morris said.

■ *Who:* Donald Judd, Robert Morris, Sol LeWitt, Carl Andre, Dan Flavin, Elsworth Kelly.
■ *When:* started in the late 1950s in the USA.

■ *Links: Abstract, Conceptual art.* Minimalism also bears some relationship to types of earlier abstract art, e.g. *De Stijl* and *Constructivism*. Sol LeWitt's drawings are a useful approach. These are always made directly onto the gallery wall, drawn not by him, but according to a set of his instructions, e.g. his 'Fifteen part drawing using four colours and all variations', 1970, Tate Modern, London. It exists only as a certificate and instructions until the Tate Modern decides to draw it upon a wall. You could research the process of your own drawing, then reduce that method down to a series of steps that could be understood and reproduced by others. Remember that the presentation of instructions is all part of the artwork.

Robert Ryman has produced a series of paintings that feature purely the colour white, e.g. 'Ledger', 1983, Tate Modern, London. White was a colour used a great deal by the Minimalists because of its associations with cleanliness and the fact that it is not actually a colour. Ad Reinhardt made paintings that were purely black, in an attempt, as he said, to present 'art as art and as nothing else' — see 'Abstract painting No. 5', 1962, Tate Modern, London. In a personal, contextual study-type unit, you could either consider whether he has succeeded in isolating art — is this possible or indeed desirable? — or examine the qualities of white or black under a series of different conditions.

■ *Formal elements:* colour, form, pattern.

modelling: there are two meanings. In painting, modelling is a way of showing three-dimensional form on a two-dimensional surface by use of light and shade. In sculpture it is the method of creating three-dimensional form by manipulating clay, plaster or other suitable media. Modelling is an additive process that builds up the form, as opposed to *carving* that takes material away, or *assemblage* that works with preformed elements.

■ *Links: form.* Rodin was recognised as one of the great modellers. Also look at Giacometti's, 'Man Pointing', 1947, Tate Modern, London.

■ *Formal elements:* form, texture.

modern/modernity: usually used to describe the new, the up-to-date and the fashionable, especially new technology. Baudelaire, the nineteenth-century French critic and poet, said 'modernity is the fleeting, the transitory, the contingent'.

■ *Links: contemporary, Modernism.*

modern art: a term, often used derogatively, to describe art that is *abstract*, or at least that the viewer does not immediately understand. Objectively the term tends to be used for art made after Impressionism, although all art is modern, i.e. new, to the person who makes it.

■ *Links: abstract, contemporary, modern, Modernism.*

Modernism/Modernist Painting: a complex term. Modernism was a period of art that could be said to run from Manet's exhibition of 'Dejeuner sur l'Herbe' and 'Olympia' at the Parisian Salon des Refusées in 1863 (see *Salon*) through to an indefinable point somewhere in the 1970s, when critics began to write about the term *Postmodernism*. Modernist art was the work made during this period that followed certain criteria:

- It took novelty (i.e. the *modern*) as one part of its subject matter, although Modernism was only partly a response to modernity.
- The second essential criterion for Modernism was art that considered its creation as its subject; art that was about itself. The high Modernist American art critic, Clement Greenberg, wrote that 'the essence of Modernism lies, as I see it, in the use of the characteristic methods of a discipline to criticise the discipline itself, not in order to subvert it but in order to entrench it more firmly within its area of competence'. Greenberg described the characteristics of painting as flatness — the flatness of the picture plane. Manet's 'Dejeuner sur l'Herbe' was one of the first paintings that so obviously made clear the way it was created, in both the sketchiness of the paint and the staged composition of the figures which referred to many other types of art that preceded it.
- The third criterion for Modernism, and therefore Modernist art, was that it was progressive — in other words, this was art that was trying to find perfection, the perfect version of a Modernist painting. If we follow Greenberg's description, the most characteristic Modernist painting would be a flat stain of colour, so that the *canvas* support was still visible and the *autographic marks* of the individual artist could also be seen.

■ *Links:* any art movement after 1860, and prefigured in most earlier nineteenth-century art. After about 1970 the grip of modernism slowly started to break, but even so, any late twentieth-century and early twenty-first century art will contain the seeds of Modernism. *Collage* was one of the great Modernist inventions, using objects from the real world so that they are both themselves and part of another work.

monochrome: a single colour or a range of tones of one colour — for example, black, white and grey.

■ *Links:* in 1954 Yves Klein painted his first monochrome painting and in 1955, working with Edouard Adam, he invented and patented his own shade of blue: 'International Klein Blue', a type of ultramarine.

mono printing/monotype: the one-off transfer of ink, or possibly thick oil paint, from a flat surface to a sheet of paper. It is a simple and spontaneous form of printing that emphasises texture and gesture. Depending on the thickness of the ink, the block is either laid ink-side up, the paper is put on top and the back of the paper is rubbed (the pressure of rubbing can be varied to create effects; Tracey Emin, for example, often uses this method) or the inked block is placed on top of the paper and they are put through a press.

The material for a block is traditionally glass or polished metal, but you can use any surface with slight texture that will take ink, e.g. wood, plastic, even a waterproof work surface. You can, for instance, build up a series of shapes from cut or torn paper which is then mounted on cardboard. Paint, or ideally ink, can then be wiped across the surface and a print taken, varying each layer according to the results and other objects and surfaces used. Mono prints can either be an image in themselves, a first sketch towards another work, or a surface that can be worked into with paint, collage, etc.

■ *When:* supposedly invented in the 1640s and used ever since.
■ *Who:* William Blake, the English artist, printer and poet, invented a variant on the mono printing process to transfer lettering onto an etching plate, so that the writing would be the right way round when printed. Edgar Degas and Paul Gauguin used mono prints in the nineteenth century.
■ *Links:* colour, pattern, texture.

montage: a form of collage in which ready-made images are assembled and mounted on a background. This differs from collage, which uses images that are not necessarily representational. Photomontage is the same method using photographs, e.g. Heartfield's 'Ten Years: Later: Father and Sons', 1924, East Berlin Academy of Arts, Germany, which, like many photomontages, is a political attack — in this case on growing German military power. Montage is also used in film, when several pieces of film are combined into one sequence.
■ *When:* since 1918.
■ *Who:* George Grosz, John Heartfield; in film, Jean Luc Godard.
■ *Links: collage, Dada.*

mosaic: a method of making very long-lasting, hard-wearing images from small cubes of stone or glass (*tesserae*) set into plaster or cement. Much used by the ancient Greeks and Romans, and a key feature of *Byzantine art.* Mosaic was an expensive medium — it takes a very long time to make and it is not possible to blend tones in mosaic easily. Once naturalism became an important feature in representing figures from the thirteenth century, fresco tended to take over as the dominant medium for wall and ceiling painting. The classic examples of mosaic work are usually thought to be Roman, e.g. Lullingstone Roman villa in Kent.
■ *Links: Art Nouveau, Byzantine art.* It is still possible to make mosaic today; you can either buy the *tesserae* ready-cut, or make them yourself with specialist shears. There are two ways of setting the *tesserae*. One method is to place them directly into the wet cement or plaster bed, the cubes face-up, so that you can see the effect and composition immediately. The other method is to make a

drawing, or *cartoon*, on a sheet of specialised, slightly sticky paper. The ***tesserae*** are placed face-down onto the paper. When the reversed image is complete, you turn the ***tesserae*** and paper over into wet cement or plaster. Each method demands certain craft skills but can be effective with practice.

multiples: three-dimensional art made, in theory, to be mass produced in large numbers and which are not part of the traditional processes for making copies, e.g. printing, cast sculptures.

■ *When:* since the 1950s, mostly in the 1960s and 1970s.

■ *Who:* Marcel Duchamp pioneered multiples with his 'boite en valise'; Claes Oldenburg's 'The Store', 1961–62, was supposed to produce multiples; Richard Hamilton, the British *Pop artist*, produced his own version, 'The Critic Smiles'.

mythology: stories of the gods and heroes, particularly from Greek and Roman sources (e.g. Ovid, see *Metamorphosis*). Mythology became an important subject for artists after the rediscovery of antiquity during the *Renaissance*.

Nabis: a group of French painters, influenced by Gauguin's colour and use of line, who combined *Symbolist* themes and a decorative style to make paintings with flat patches of colour and heavy outlines and edges, e.g. Paul Sérusier's 'Bois d'Amour at Pont-Aven', 1888, Musée d'Orsay, Paris. They are also called the Pont-Aven School.

■ *When:* the 1890s.

■ *Who:* Paul Sérusier, Pierre Bonnard, Maurice Denis, Edouard Vuillard.

■ *Links: cloissonisme, Post-Impressionism, Symbolism.*

■ *Formal elements:* colour, line, pattern.

naïve painting: self-taught art in Western societies not influenced by academic traditions (scale or linear perspective, for instance). Naïve art is driven by narrative, often the intense personal fantasies of the artist.

■ *When:* developed in the nineteenth century and gaining recognition in the early twentieth century.

■ *Who:* Henri Rousseau was the great favourite of the Parisian *avant-garde* in the early twentieth century, e.g. 'Tropical Storm with a Tiger', 1891, National Gallery, London. Also the Cornishman, Alfred Wallis, e.g. 'The Hold House Port Mear Square Island Port Mear Beach', 1932, Tate St Ives, Cornwall, whose small paintings on odd-shaped pieces of card, showing child-like images of houses and boats, heavily influenced the Modernist artists of St Ives.

■ *Links: Art Brut, primitivism.*

■ *Formal elements:* all.

narrative: a work of art that tells a story. Narrative was the major function of art until Cubism made the subject matter the story of the creation of the object itself.

■ *Links: ideal, mythology, Renaissance.*

naturalism: see *realism*.

Nazi/National Socialist art: the only art permitted in the Third Reich by Adolf Hitler. This was 'racially conscious' propaganda designed to promote the Aryan race by its glorification of stereotypes: noble heroes, peasant life and wholesome families; blond supermen and women working for the glory of the Motherland. National Socialist art used many of the traditions of *history painting;* it was large, smoothly painted, with no evidence of the artist's brushstrokes. Other Modernist movements were attacked as 'degenerate', art was destroyed and the artists persecuted. Nazi art, like fascist art in Italy, depended on a stripped-down neo-classical style — this meant that the neo-classical style was often associated with the horrors of fascism and the Holocaust and, as a result, was little used after the Second World War (see *abstract*).

■ *When:* 1933–45.

■ *Who:* Adolf Ziegler, Josef Thorak.

■ *Links: history painting, ideal.* For an alternative to Nazi art, see *Bauhaus* for the sort of 'degenerate art' closed down by the Nazis. Although the paintings and sculpture are of low quality, the films of Leni Reifenstahl, e.g. *Triumph of the Will,* have often been plundered for imagery by advertisers — if you see beautiful blond young men in sporting poses photographed in black and white, Reifenstahl's work is probably the inspiration.

negative space: the areas between objects — an important but often forgotten element of any visual analysis. In making a drawing of a group of objects, we concentrate on the objects themselves, but to analyse their *form* we need to find the three-dimensional space these objects occupy.

■ *Links: form.* Rachel Whiteread, the British artist associated with the *YBAs*, casts the spaces inside objects, for instance 'Untitled (One Hundred Spaces)', 1995, Arts Council, Great Britain. These are casts in translucent resin of the gaps underneath chairs and stools, the sort of negative space we usually ignore. Negative space or the unregarded areas between objects is a fertile area for making drawings and could be a useful *theme* to investigate. What have other artists done with this idea? Consider, for instance, the classic exercise of making monochrome drawings of the spaces between a stack of stools or chairs. Use white chalk on black paper and, without using any *tone*, draw the negative spaces; the untouched black paper will reveal the objects. For the next step, look at late Cézanne watercolours, e.g. 'Still Life with Green Melon', 1902–06, Private Collection. Notice that there is no sharp *turning edge* to the melon, but a repeated blue contour that moves into the space of the glass next to it; the gap between the two objects is full of their *colour* relationships.

Neo-: a prefix attached to a word to mean a new form of, and therefore a type of, revival, as in *Neo-classicism* — a new version of *Classical* art.

Neo-classicism: a style of art and architecture in Europe which developed in reaction to *Rococo* and the *Baroque*. Archaeological discoveries at Pompeii in 1748 showed artists exactly what ancient Roman art looked like and, unlike

Renaissance artists, Neo-classical artists were able to imitate *Classical* art, architecture and sculpture exactly for the first time. Neo-classicism was characterised by clear colours, sharp lines, and figures arranged in *ideal* gestures, e.g. David's 'The Oath of the Horatii', 1784, Musée du Louvre, Paris, where the three brothers swear a heroic oath as their father lifts their swords to the gods. The composition copies the frieze-like arrangement familiar from classical temples. The painted architecture is accurate, as are the costumes and the armour, and even the faces and the shapes of the men's noses.

■ *When:* eighteenth and nineteenth centuries.

■ *Who:* Jaques Louis David, Angelica Kauffmann, Jean Auguste Dominique Ingres.

■ *Links:* *history painting, ideal, Nazi art, Renaissance.* During the nineteenth century Neo-classicism was seen as the opposite of *Gothic*, in what was called the 'Battle of the Styles'. Try comparing their relevant characteristics and measuring them against the work you want to make.

Neo-Impressionism: see *divisionism.*

Neo-Plasticism: see *De Stijl.*

Non-Objective art: a term used for the purest forms of *abstract* art, that have no reference to the process of *abstraction* from nature and are purely *formal* arrangements of colour.

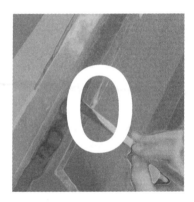

objet trouvé: see *found object*.

oeuvre: the complete works of an artist.

oil paint: pigments bound with oil, usually linseed. Although the medium predates him, oil paint was probably first used in its present form by Jan van Eyck in the Netherlands. It reached *Renaissance* Italy via northern artists working in Naples and then worked its way back north. The important technical quality of oil paint is that it dries slowly, unlike the previously dominant *medium*, **tempera**, which dried very quickly. This meant that oil paint could be reworked whilst still wet, and layers of thin paint or *glazes* could be built onto underpainting to mimic surfaces, especially skin. Oil paint blends easily, its shine being given by the oil, and the fact that it can be applied in translucent layers means that deeper *colours* can be built up. Soft colours and textures, the luminous sheen of bright highlighting, the soft fold of cloth shown by blending a darker *tone* for the shadow against the lighter tone for the highlight, these are all made possible by the technical qualities of oil paint. Oil paintings were easier to preserve than frescoes and did not need the perfectly smooth surface of a wooden panel. After about 1500 the Venetians applied their colour direct to *canvas*, a more convenient surface than wood, which rotted or warped in the damp air. Canvases could be made up to the size of murals and could be rolled up and transported or exported.

■ *When:* since its first appearance in the early fifteenth century, oil paint has been a crucial medium for painting.

By the seventeenth century the practice of painting entirely with oils and varnishes was the norm, and had become very sophisticated, particularly in the careful application of layers of thinned paint to represent the action of light on a wide variety of surfaces (see *glazes*). The invention of the metal paint tube in 1841, first manufactured in London by Windsor and Newton, freed artists from the studio and allowed them to use oil paint outdoors (see *Impressionism*). They no longer needed to grind their own colours and, as

O

artificial pigments came onto the market, they could now use vivid colour in some quantity. This set the stage for radical changes in the use of oil paint, as artists painted directly onto the canvas in solid, powerful blocks of colour (see *Post-Impressionism*).

■ *Who:* oil paint was traditionally supposed to have been invented by Jan van Eyck in Holland. This is almost certainly not true, as linseed and nut oil had been used since the Middle Ages as a medium for pigments. However, van Eyck and his contemporaries in the early fifteenth century did make important experiments with oil paint glazes over an under-layer of opaque egg *tempera* paint that led to the further development of the method in Italy. Later artists, e.g. Titian and, after him, El Greco, Rubens and Velasquez, used a brown pigmented ground on their canvases, which allowed them to leave some areas unpainted. The brown areas could provide contrasting texture and subtle half-tones when glazed. Rembrandt used a much darker ground so that his paintings are filled with warm tones, whereas the *Pre-Raphaelites* in the nineteenth century worked their oil paint into a wet, white ground, which gave brilliant colours with a sharp focus. The first half of the twentieth century probably marked the final stages of the dominance of oil paint — the invention of *acrylic* in the 1960s posed a great challenge, for example, as did the use of non-art paint such as the household enamels which Jackson Pollock used. But it is noticeable that with artists who make paintings — Frank Auerbach, Gillian Ayres, Lucian Freud, Howard Hodgkin, Gerhard Richter and many more — oil paint is still a favourite medium.

■ *Links:* *glaze, illusion, impasto, Renaissance.* Compare two examples of oil painting, one from the Renaissance, e.g. Titian's 'Bachus and Ariadne' 1522–32, National Gallery, London, which is a classic use of rich oil paint and glazes to build up strong colours and the illusion of three-dimensional form, with the American *Abstract Expressionist* artist, Clyfford Still's '1953', 1953, Tate Modern, London. This is a large, mostly vivid blue, painting, with flashes of red (the *complementary* colour to blue) in the bottom left-hand corner and a jagged area of yellow and purple in the upper right. How are these two artists using the colour blue? Notice that Still does not use transparent glazes, although the blue is *scumbled* onto a darker layer underneath. Is the lack of glazing a conscious attempt to move away from the illusionistic skills of earlier oil painting, such as the Titian? If you have access to oil paints, you could make a series of visual research pieces based on an analysis of these two paintings, their aims and functions. It would be a good idea to widen the range to include *tempera* and fresco, to show the qualities of oil paint and how they affect the subsequent work, e.g. Duccio's *triptych* of 'Virgin and Child with St Dominic and St Aurea', 1310–20, National Gallery, London, *tempera* on wood, with Giotto's frescos in the Arena Chapel, Padua, 1305.

Unless you can work in a dedicated studio, have somewhere to store wet artwork and can easily change your clothes, oil paint is not always a suitable medium for schools and colleges, as it tends to spread everywhere. Oil paint is not soluble in water and therefore difficult, if not impossible, to get out of uniforms or good clothes. White spirit, the medium for cleaning brushes and palettes, smells strongly and does not mix well with other paints and brushes in the ordinary art department sink. That said, oil paint is a wonderful, if expensive, medium, allowing years of happy experimentation.

■ *Formal elements:* all except perhaps line.

Op art: an abstract art based on geometric, often monochrome, patterns with sharp, well defined edges that trick the eye to create after-images, and look as though they are moving, or throbbing, e.g. Bridget Riley, 'Hesitate', 1964, Tate Britain, London.

■ *When:* in the 1960s.

■ *Who:* Josef Albers, who was an early pioneer of optical effects through geometric pattern (see *Bauhaus*), Bridget Riley, Victor Vasarely. Op art was also very important for 1960s' fashion — Bridget Riley tried to sue an American company that used one of her paintings on a dress fabric.

■ *Links:* illusion, Kinetic art, Pop art.

■ *Formal elements:* pattern.

optical mixing: see *divisionism.*

organic: in artistic terms organic means art work in which the forms shown seem to derive from a study of nature: for instance, curving shapes that indicate growth, e.g. Jean Arp's 'Pagoda Fruit' of 1949, Tate Modern, London, which is a bronze sculpture of two rounded, abstract shapes, whose forms suggest seed pods, shells, strange fruit — certainly something natural, or organic. Art critics use the term 'organic' to describe the composition of an artwork that looks balanced — 'the organic whole'. *Art Nouveau*, the decorative style in the arts, and particularly architecture, that swept across Europe from the end of the nineteenth century to the First World War, was probably the most coherent example of using organic form as the starting point for an entire movement. Art Nouveau used asymmetrical shapes, lines and forms that came ultimately from plants, e.g. the curving capitals of the supporting columns of Victor Horta's Hotel Tassel, Brussels, 1892–93, have iron tendrils that flow upwards to the metal structures above, far more reminiscent of growing ivy than the functional part of a building.

Orphism/Orphic Cubism: a type of painting which developed out of *Cubism* practised by Robert Delaunay and his associates. They used strong colour and images of Paris (the Eiffel Tower in particular, although there is a painting by Robert Delaunay on the unlikely subject of Cardiff Football Club!). Orphists also developed some of the first abstract imagery using musical themes, e.g. Delaunay's 'Circular Forms, Sun and Moon', 1912–13, Kunsthaus, Zurich, Switzerland. The poet Guillaume Apollinaire coined the term, in reference to Orpheus, the singer and poet in Greek mythology, as the artists wanted to introduce lyricism to the austere Cubist style. Through experimentation their subject matter became abstract.

■ *When:* 1911–14, limited to Paris.

■ *Who:* Robert and Sonia Delaunay, Marcel Duchamp, Fernand Léger and Francis Picabia.

■ *Links: Cubism.* Paul Klee visited Delaunay in 1912 and his subsequent art was influenced by the Orphic use of colour (see *Bauhaus*).

orthogonals: creating the illusion of depth on a flat surface (*picture plane*). Using *perspective* depends on the notion that parallel lines meet at infinity. Those receding parallels perpendicular to the picture plane are the orthogonals, which draw the viewer's eye towards the *vanishing point* and make the illusion of the pavement (see *perspective*) that characterises the pictorial space of most *Renaissance* paintings.

■ *Links: Cubism, foreshortening, perspective, Renaissance.*

Outsider art: see *Art Brut.*

palette: a tray or flat surface, usually oval or kidney-shaped, on which an artist mixes paints. It also means the colours used by an artist, i.e. a range of colours particular to an artist or a piece of artwork.

■ *Links: colour, monochrome.* See *Cubism* for examples of a restricted palette and *Post-Impressionism* for examples of a heightened palette.

panel painting: the term for painting on a flat support that is rigid and can be moved around, in contrast to *fresco*. Until the fifteenth century the support was generally a wooden panel, although copper was also used in the Netherlands. In the Middle Ages leather was often stretched over panels. Panels were increasingly replaced by *canvas*, which was stretched over a frame.

pastel: a drawing medium consisting of ground pigment mixed with gum or resin to make a usable stick. Unlike the decorating term 'pastel' which usually means pale colours, pastels make strong, bright colour with a slight *impasto* texture. Pastels' strength is their directness — there is no mixing with water or other media, and you can build up a coloured surface and complete forms very quickly. The individual drawn mark can be contrasted against a large area, either flat or blended, although pastel cannot really be used in more than one or two layers, as the surface becomes clogged. Pastels tend to come in three grades: soft, medium and hard — the soft is the easiest to use. Paper or canvas will need to have a reasonable tooth (see *ground*) to catch the pastel — the rougher the ground the more of it will show through. Pastels can be blended with the end of a finger, or a rag. White spirit will dissolve the pastel slightly to make wash-like effects (you can do the same thing with cheap wax crayons). The finished works are fragile and fixative sprays tend to discolour the pigments.

■ *When:* first used in Italy in the sixteenth century; the high point is probably Degas in the nineteenth century.

■ *Links: autographic mark, colour, drawing.* Look also at Degas' 'After the Bath, Woman Drying Herself', 1895, Courtauld Gallery, London — a drawing, in that you can see a series of individual strokes of colour as Degas tries to find the form in front of him, but also a finished piece of art. There is a directness that comes from the artist working straight from the model, but also an organised composition, with a diagonal travelling from left to right, balanced by the horizontal bath. At least three different methods of applying pastel have been used here: with a brush, almost liquid, and as a drawing stick. Notice the effect of strong complementary strokes of colour. Try experimenting yourself.

■ *Formal elements:* all.

patina: the colouring of the surface of a metal object as it ages, particularly of *bronze*, which develops an attractive green colouring.

■ *Links:* sculpture.

■ *Formal elements:* colour, pattern, texture.

patron/patronage: someone who continually buys an artist's work, or pays for expenses while the art is being made. The *Renaissance* was the beginning of the move from state or church patronage to art bought by individuals. Lorenzo di Medici, for instance, was the major Florentine patron. Patronage is important, because whoever buys the work will have views on what it looks like, and will sponsor art that appeals to them or promotes their views. The question of patronage still exists today — Charles Saatchi is the major patron of British art (see *YBAs*) and his taste currently dominates the London art world.

Performance art: a form of action-based art, using theatre, music, film, video, etc. Performance is based on a fixed choreography — unlike the *Happening*, it is not improvised or based on audience participation.

■ *When:* from the mid-1970s onwards, although, like the Happening, its roots are probably in *Futurism* and *Dada*.

■ *Links: Pop art, shock.* Gilbert and George, the living British sculptors (see *YBAs*), began as performance artists. A student work in 1967 involved painting themselves bronze and standing on a table for 8 hours singing *Underneath the Arches*. Another early work, 'Gordon's Gets us Drunk', filmed the two artists in a London pub as Gordon's gin did just that. Like many other performances, copying this work is not recommended.

perspective: the system for representing three-dimensional objects on a two-dimensional surface, creating the *illusion* of spatial depth. Linear perspective is mathematically based on a fixed viewpoint with one eye closed, and therefore different from the binocular vision of the moving head that is simultaneously linked to information provided by all the other senses. Perspective was scientifically explained in the *Renaissance* and applied to painting. In central perspective the flat, vertical surface of the picture (*picture plane*) is imagined to be at right angles to the parallel lines (*orthogonals*) that run into the depth of the painting and meet at infinity, the vanishing point, creating a chessboard or pavement upon which to construct the illusion of organised pictorial space. By using *foreshortening*, objects grow smaller the further they are away. *Aerial perspective*, invented by Leonardo da Vinci, creates the illusion of depth in painting by making objects and areas lose their colour intensity, become hazy (**sfumato**), and look bluer the further away they are.

■ *When:* although basic perspective systems existed in antiquity, it was Brunelleschi, the architect of the Cathedral dome in Florence, who first used linear perspective in about 1415, using precise measurements to establish the basic system for translating actual spatial relationships to their proportional equivalents in paint. In his book, *On Painting*, 1425, Leon Battisa Alberti put together the rules for using a basic single viewpoint perspective.

■ *Who:* every artist since Brunelleschi.

■ *Links:* the Florentine Early *Renaissance* artist, Tommaso Masaccio, painted one of the first believable 'holes in the wall' — a fresco using linear perspective — 'The Holy Trinity', 1427, Santa Maria Novella, Florence. The perspective in this work divides the pictorial space into two areas: spiritual and temporal. Compare the Masaccio fresco with other works, e.g. the post-*Cubist*, *Orphic* painting by Robert Delaunay, 'The Red Tower', 1911–12, Solomon R. Guggenheim Museum, New York, which took the *Cubist* notion that a painting could include all the possible ideas about a subject, not just the limited 'Renaissance' version of what it looks like from a frontal static position. Compare this with, perhaps, the British artist Gary Hume (see *YBAs*) and his angel paintings, e.g. 'Yellow Angels' 1999, Mathew Marks Gallery, New York, which superimposes a series of drawings, rather than creating illusionistic depth, as had been the task of perspective up until 1907.

photomontage: see *montage*.

photorealism: figurative art copied very accurately from photographs, mostly in reaction to the dominant artistic form of abstract painting. It developed from *Pop art*, particularly in its appeal to popular rather than *fine art* taste. Photorealism raised the status of the photograph to a subject in itself, although as an idea rather than the actual practice of photography. Photorealist images are characterised by very sharply focused, precise imagery, unlike photographs, which have a field of focus, i.e. some parts will be blurry. In other words, these images are about the concept of the photo (see *Conceptual art*) rather than the actual object — we do not, for instance, see the glare of light you get from the surface of an ordinary glossy snap.

■ *When:* from 1970.

■ *Who:* Chuck Close, Richard Estes.

■ *Links: Pop art.* Like the photos they copy, photorealist images flatten the range of tones and, importantly as a reaction against *Abstract Expressionism*, the textures. This means that these works can be seen as purely *formal* images, i.e. abstract works; just a range of colours on a surface. Many of the artists turned their works upside down as they made them, so that they would not be tempted to interpret the subject as they worked; this is a technique you might wish to explore.

picture plane: the flat surface, e.g. *canvas, panel* or paper, on which two-dimensional art is made. In linear *perspective* the picture plane is often referred to as a fourth wall. The *Renaissance* artist, architect and writer Alberti described the workings of perspective in 1435, and called the vertical picture plane 'a window between the viewer and the view shown in the painting'.
■ *Links: Renaissance.*

picturesque: literally looking like a picture, a term used to describe landscape in England in the eighteenth century. It became a standard of taste. This was the period of landscape gardening, when landowners employed men like Capability Brown to remodel their country estates entirely to look like the art they admired, e.g. Claude's 'Marriage of Isaac and Rebekah', 1648, National Gallery, London.
■ *When:* eighteenth and nineteenth centuries.
■ *Links: Land art, landscape, Romanticism.*

Pietà/Deposition/Lamentation: the image of the grieving Virgin Mary with the body of Christ, her son, usually across her knees — the point in the Christian *narrative* after the crucifixion when she is alone with her dead son. If she is grieving with others it can be known as 'the Lamentation'. All three images show the lowest point of the story, before the Resurrection.

The Deposition, which happens earlier in the narrative than the **Pietà**, shows the lowering of Christ's body from the cross, usually by many characters including the Virgin Mary, Mary Magdalen, St John the Evangelist, Nicodemus (who supplied the ointments to preserve the body) and Joseph of Arimathea (who, according to some mythologies, brought the young Christ to Britain). Often the Deposition shows a skull, representing Golgotha, the hill of skulls where Christ was sacrificed.
■ *Links:* Michelangelo's marble sculpture of the 'Pietà', 1498–99, St Peter's, Rome, solves the technical problem of how to place a grown (if dead) man across the knees of a woman. Michelangelo takes the northern European image of the Pietà and, by bending Christ's limbs to echo the Virgin's shape, and with his great skill in sculpting the folds of cloth, makes Christ's body appear longer and bigger than it actually is. Michelangelo sculpted this work at the age of 23, when he was making his name and proving himself. It is the only work that he signed and his signature is prominently placed on the belt across Mary's

chest. (Young men showing off are a constant theme throughout the history of art: think of the *Cubists* or even the *YBAs*.)

Rogier van der Weyden's 'The Descent from the Cross', 1435, Museo del Prado, Madrid, is a northern European version of the Deposition theme set in a very shallow pictorial space; the shape of the Virgin Mary's falling body exactly follows that of her son. St John on one side and Mary Magdalene on the other create curving shapes to return the eye to the centre; large figures arranged in a constricted space emphasise the emotional impact.

■ *Formal elements:* all.

plastic: capable of being moulded or shaped — a descriptive term used before the invention of the material we now call plastic. The 'plastic arts' means the modelling or representation of solid objects, particularly used by the *De Stijl* group, who also described their art as Neo-Plasticism.

***plein air* painting:** see *Impressionism*.

pointillism: see *divisionism* for greater detail. Late *Impressionist* (*Neo-Impressionist*) stylistic movement which juxtaposes colours in little brushstrokes or points, so that the *optical mix* occurs in the eye of the viewer, and not on the painter's *palette*.

■ *Link:* Ben Day process, divisionism.

polyptych: a picture or relief, usually an altarpiece, made up of more than three separate panels folded or hinged together.

■ *Links:* diptych and triptych.

Pop art: movement based on the images of popular culture and consumerism. Pop art started in Britain and America at roughly the same time. Pop was defined by the British artist, Richard Hamilton, as: 'Popular/Transient/Expendable/Low cost/Mass produced/Young/Witty/Sexy/Gimmicky/Glamorous/Big business'. The first Pop art work was probably Hamilton's 'Just What is it that Makes Today's Homes so Different, so Appealing?', 1956, Collection Edward Janss, Jr, Thousand Oaks, California. This was a *collage* full of contemporary images — the ceiling is a photograph of the surface of the moon, Al Jolson advertises *The Jazz Singer*, the first film to combine speech and images, the carpet is a photograph by the New York photogapher Weegee of Coney Island — but it is no coincidence that it also looks like an *Abstract Expressionist* painting. Pop was a deliberate reaction against the *fine art* approach to making art, especially of the Abstract Expressionists, and a celebration of all things *modern*, particularly if they were American.

Pop art used the images of consumerist society, mostly advertising, for example Warhol's famous '200 Campbell's Soup Cans', 1962, Private Collection, New York, rather than the traditional *Genres* of art, still life, landscape, etc. Pop art took the visual characteristics of the modern world, e.g. Lichtenstein's comic book painting 'Whaam', 1963, Tate Modern, London, where he painted the *Ben Day dots* of the printing process onto huge canvases, turning them into high art.

■ *When:* from the late 1950s to the end of the 1960s.

■ *Who:* in the USA: Jasper Johns, Roy Lichtenstein, Claes Oldenburg, Robert Rauschenberg, Andy Warhol; in the UK: Richard Hamilton, David Hockney, Peter Blake.

■ *Links: Ben Day process, collage. Dada* used everyday things in art — look also at Duchamp's *ready-mades* for a way of taking real objects and making them art. Pop was sometimes called Neo-Dada, particularly the early work of Jasper Johns and Robert Rauschenberg. See also *montage* and *screen printing*.

Lichtenstein's comic images were taken from war or love comics. Since the Second World War, America had already fought in Korea and was about to become disastrously involved in Vietnam. Jasper Johns had made many drawings and paintings of the American flag, e.g. ' Three Flags', 1958, Whitney Museum, New York. Although these images do not obviously comment on their subject, they make a commentary of sorts on issues of the period. If you are making work inspired by Pop art, think carefully about the imagery you use and its relationship to your own period; see *Zeitgeist*. What are the visual characteristics of the mass media you see around you now? What, for example, are the features of back-lit computer screens that you can use in your work? What about pixillation and digitised images? Remember that you are not merely copying the world around you; your task is to analyse it visually, making sure, of course, that all your analysis is recorded in your work journal in a suitable visual style.

■ *Formal elements:* all except perhaps texture.

portrait: the image and likeness of a person in a drawing, painting, photograph or sculpture. One of the *Genres* of art, there are many types of portrait with different functions: self-portraits, an individual person, double and group portraits. 'Portrait' is also the term we use for the shape of a rectangular piece of paper so that the longest side is vertical — the alternative is 'landscape'.

post-: a prefix which means after or following. In art terms it often signifies a reaction against — e.g. *Post-Impressionism* happened after *Impressionism*.

Post-Impressionism: term used to describe the work of French artists who moved away from *Impressionism*, in particular Cézanne, Gauguin, Matisse and van Gogh. Impressionist painting aimed to be a purely optical response to the subject matter, i.e. painting only what can be seen. This denied the symbolic nature of art and the possibility that a painting could be a personal and emotional response. Impressionist techniques attempted to capture the envelope of light around an object and in the atmosphere, which made creating solid pictorial form difficult. Post-Impressionism began the move away from this *naturalism*. Although there was no organised group of Post-Impressionists, these four key artists all reacted against Impressionism, trying to make an art that concentrated on the powerful representation of *form*. Cézanne said that he wanted to 'make of Impressionism something solid and enduring, like that of the museums'. Van Gogh and Gauguin especially searched for an art that could have a symbolic as well as an optical content — they formed the link between Impressionism and *Expressionism*.

■ *When:* 1880–1905.

■ *Who:* Paul Cézanne, Paul Gauguin, Henri Matisse, Vincent van Gogh.

■ *Links:* these four artists were the major inspiration for most of the early twentieth-century art movements. Between them they were largely responsible for what we call *modern art*. Cézanne's work on pictorial form was crucial for Picasso and Braque and subsequently *Cubism*, the early versions of which could well be called Cézannism. Gauguin's investigations of *Symbolism* in Brittany and *primitivism* in Tahiti, and van Gogh's use of power and colour, led to *Fauvism* and *Expressionism*, to recognising that personal emotion can be a suitable subject for art.

■ *Formal elements:* colour, form, texture.

Postmodernism: a term originally taken from architecture, but subsequently applied to the rest of the arts and popular culture. *Modernism* was a progressive move towards art that was overwhelmingly abstract — one single style that rejected all preceding artistic traditions. Postmodernism insisted that art could and should build on all the art that came before and that everyone should be able to understand it. What this tended to produce was a series of witty, knowing quotes rather than anything new — for instance, Philip Johnson's 'A T and T Building', 1979, New York, which is essentially an old-fashioned, plain, rectangular skyscraper, but on the top is a pediment taken from a piece of *Neo-classical* furniture, in theory mixing two different styles. Postmodernism is probably not important in itself, the work is mostly another form of montage, but if it signalled the end of Modernism the question is: what happens now?

■ *When:* since the 1970s, but probably over now.

■ *Who:* architects: Charles Jencks, Robert Venturi.

■ *Links:* collage, Modernism.

Pre-Raphaelites/the Pre-Raphaelite Brotherhood: a group of English artists who believed that Italian painting before Raphael was the best model. Pre-Raphaelite paintings had strong moral subjects and were always worked directly from nature in a very sharp, minutely-detailed style, e.g. Holman Hunt's 'The Awakening Conscience', 1853, Tate Britain, London. From about the 1860s some artists started painting medieval themes, which continued well into the twentieth century, e.g. Edward Burne-Jones' 'King Cophetua and the Beggar Maid', 1884, Tate Britain, London. The subject matter of Pre-Raphaelite painting was mainly literary, with a serious intent, using Shakespeare, poetry and the Bible as inspiration. The aim was to find new images to replace the old worn-out ones, to find new symbols and allegories to represent the truth in ancient stories and myths. They also painted contemporary subjects, e.g. Holman Hunt's 'The Awakening Conscience', 1853–54, Tate Britain, London, an image of a young mistress realising that she should change her life by leaving her lover. The couple in the painting are surrounded by what look like ordinary domestic objects, but which in this context can be read as symbols of the girl's position — she has realised her mistake in being a 'kept woman' and resolves to live a 'better' life in the future.

■ *When:* 1848–1860s.

■ *Who:* John Everett Millais, William Holman Hunt, Dante Gabriel Rossetti.

■ *Links: allegory, Arts and Crafts movement, figurative, realism, Renaissance.*

■ *Formal elements:* all.

primary colours: the colours red, yellow and blue, which cannot be made by mixing other colours. All other colours are produced by mixing primary colours.

■ *Links: colour, complementary colours, divisionism, secondary colours.*

primitivism: there are several meanings. In the nineteenth century 'primitive' meant art from non-Western and Eastern societies, which was seen as less developed and unsophisticated in comparison with the West in particular. Primitivism now tends to refer to a search for art that has not been 'corrupted' by Western civilisation and is therefore somehow more 'authentic' — hence, for example, Gauguin's journey to Tahiti in the 1890s (see *Post-Impressionism*) or the deliberate crudeness of the figures in the painting of the *Expressionists*.

Another sense is the twentieth century's use of the word to describe art of simple imagery that has not been *modelled* in the traditional *Renaissance* manner. For instance, the treatment of the figures in Picasso's 'Les Demoiselles d'Avignon', 1907, Museum of Modern Art, New York, was largely inspired by his study of African and Iberian masks on display in the Musée du Louvre.

■ *Links: naïve painting, woodcut.*

■ *Formal elements:* colour, form, pattern, texture.

quattrocento: Italian term for the fifteenth century, especially art and literature.

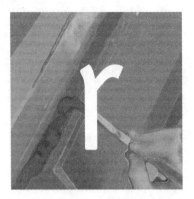

ready-made: little changed, industrially-produced objects that were declared 'works of art' by the artist Marcel Duchamp. It is the combination of the act of choosing and their exhibition in a gallery that makes a previously ordinary object become a work of art — a ready-made.

■ *When:* 1913–45.

■ *Who:* a name introduced by Marcel Duchamp in 1913, the first ready-made was probably the 'assisted ready-made' of the bicycle wheel mounted on a kitchen stool (see *bicycle*). The most famous ready-made was possibly 'Fountain', 1917 (original lost, copies in Museum of Modern Art, New York, and Tate Modern, London). Signed with a made-up name, R. Mutt (makers of sanitary ware), and submitted to an art competition in America, 'Fountain' was an ordinary gentleman's urinal. By taking a mass-produced object and merely adding a title, Duchamp was producing a ready-made sculpture. This was a way of not only pointing out the intellectual basis for art and moving attention away from the physical process of creating it ('I wanted to put painting once more at the service of the mind') but also asking questions about the fundamental nature of art and the way it is exhibited. The influence of Duchamp's ready-mades was considerable — the introduction of the witty *shock* to the viewer, critic and art authorities, and the insistence that the intellectual and philosophical side of art need not be accompanied by a lovingly-crafted object, had a profound effect on the subsequent history of art.

■ *Links: Conceptual art, Dada, found object, YBAs.*

realism: both a style and a particular movement in art. As a style, realism (with a small 'r') is similar to naturalism — art based on a close study of nature and the representation of the world, which has been the aim of many artists since the ancient Egyptians. Carried to one conclusion, this can result in the search for ideal rather than actual forms, and the celebration of craft skills (e.g. *trompe l'oeil* — see *illusion*) rather than the visual analysis of the world. It is a method that often uses imitation of the photograph, rather than the eye, as the measure of success.

Realism (with a capital 'R') does not mean the naturalistic representation of people and places (see above) but a celebration of the ordinary and everyday, in other words the opposite of the *ideal*. The key Realist figure, Gustave Courbet, refused to paint angels until he had actually seen one. Realism was an art about 'modern' life; for example Courbet's painting 'A Burial at Ornans' 1849–50, Musée d'Orsay, Paris. A painting big enough to be considered a *history painting*, it clearly had something important to say and was trying to rival great art of the past. Yet the subject is the ordinary people of a small town in France, dressed in black. Some even have red noses, no one is looking directly at the viewer and we have no idea who is being buried. In other words, the painting is not composed in the traditional sense. The central subject of the painting is a hole in the ground, it has no mythology, no aristocratic or grand figures from the past and the predominant colours are dark and grubby — 'the heroism of modern life', as the critic Baudelaire called it.

■ *When:* 1845–80.

■ *Who:* Gustave Courbet, Edouard Manet.

■ *Links: photorealism, Pre-Raphaelites, Romanticism.* In many ways *Impressionism* was a continuation of Realism, with a lighter palette and greater painterliness. Try investigating the aims of both movements, particularly Degas, who is often called a Realist, and comparing the results.

■ *Formal elements:* all.

relief: a raised three-dimensional surface in sculpture. A sculpture carved from a flat surface so that only a small part of it projects is described as low relief (or bas relief); if a great deal of it sticks out it is called high relief.

relief printing: a method of printing. The most familiar is lino-cut, where the ink is held on the raised surface of the block. In other words, what is cut away does not print, unlike ***intaglio*** printing where the ink remains in the grooves.

■ *Links: engraving, etching, woodcut.*

■ *Formal elements:* colour, pattern, texture.

Renaissance: the art, culture, science and spirit of a period which began in the fourteenth century in Italy. It marked the waning of the Middle Ages and the rise of the modern world. The High Renaissance generally represents the art that most people associate with this period, i.e. Michelangelo's 'David', his Sistine Chapel ceiling, Leonardo da Vinci's 'Mona Lisa', Raphael's 'School of Athens' fresco and so on. The Renaissance is split into two periods: the Early Renaissance, usually said to begin with Giotto (see both *fresco* and *Gothic*) centring on Florence, and the High Renaissance, based in Rome, with the great names of Leonardo da Vinci, Michelangelo, Raphael and Titian, lasting until the sack of Rome in 1527. These definitions are fairly arbitrary.

The key points about this whole period fundamental to the shaping of Western society are:

- the revival of interest in *Classical* forms and knowledge
- the development of humanist ideals and the scientific approach
- the raising of the status of artists from mere craftsmen to the equals of princes, and the engines of cultural change

Classical sculpture provided the inspiration for the *ideal* naked human form that became the standard from the Renaissance onwards. Although little classical painting was known, writing about it still existed, and artists and their public read stories retold by Pliny, such as Zeuxis and the grapes (see *illusion*), and learnt that painting should be as naturalistic as possible (see *realism*) and should be a search for an ideal form. Classical architecture was more abundant and architects could use these models for accuracy, and continued to do so until the late nineteenth century (see *Neo-classicism*). The invention, or strictly speaking, the revival and refinement, of the classical method of *perspective* started with Brunelleschi, architect of the Cathedral dome in Florence — a great symbol of the triumph of Renaissance science and classical learning.

The legacies of the Renaissance are various and pervasive: the assumption that painting should consist of heroic figures based loosely on classical models, operating in a three-dimensional picture space, was the foundation of all painting thereafter. It was in fact so fundamental that it was not questioned until the second half of the nineteenth century some 400 years later. Painters owe to the Renaissance *oil paint*, the major medium for their work, unrivalled until the invention of *acrylic*.

The development of oil paint started in the Netherlands. There was as much of a Renaissance in northern Europe as in Italy, particularly through the influence of Albrecht Dürer, who had travelled to Italy, e.g. 'Self Portrait at 28', 1500, Alte Pinakotheck, Munich, which shows the artist in the image of Christ. At first sight this seems an astonishingly arrogant assumption, but it underlines perhaps the most important cultural legacy of the Renaissance — humanism. Humanism is the study of God through his creations and it developed from a renewed interest in the classical past, which led to a quest for a new set of values and standards to judge not only art work, but behaviour and success. So, for example, ability was more important than birth, a person could be valued for their contribution rather than their status. The Renaissance was the beginning of the modern age and of the individual, either artist, poet, merchant or writer.

■ *When:* Early Renaissance 1420–1500; High Renaissance 1500–27.

- **Who:** too many to mention, but the obvious names are Brunelleschi, Donatello, Dürer, Giotto, Leonardo da Vinci, Masaccio, Michelangelo, Raphael.
- **Links:** *Classicism*. *Mannerism* and then the *Baroque* are the two art movements that developed after the Renaissance. *Modernism*, and *Cubism* in particular, are normally described as the first major attempts to reject Renaissance forms and methods.
- **Formal elements:** all.

repoussoir: a figure or object set in the foreground of a painting in order to frame the mid- and background and create pictorial depth. In *landscapes*, for instance, artists often use a tree. It is a term that not only need apply to landscapes but can also describe *abstract* work — for example Willem de Kooning's 'Door to the River', 1960, Whitney Museum of American Art, New York. The yellow strokes on the left and at the top act as framing devices — they lead the eye into the *composition*. In other words, moving from a bright *foreground* to a darker *background* creates depth, and is the usual method of constructing a landscape.

- **Links:** *composition, landscape*. If you want to apply this form of composition to your own work, you could make an *annotated* version of an older landscape painting, e.g. Claude's 'The Marriage of Isaac and Rebekah', 1648, National Gallery, London. Compare this composition with an annotated version of a more recent work, e.g. the de Kooning above, and with an annotated version of your own work. Point out the similarities and differences between the three works and use this knowledge to plan the composition of your final piece.

Rococo: a decorative style originating in France in about 1700, during the reign of Louis XV — see, for example, Fragonard's 'The Swing', 1767, Wallace Collection, London, a painting full of the gentle swirling shapes of a young woman's dress, echoed in the forms of the trees around her. At her feet a young man is placed in such a way that he can see under the billowing skirts. Rococo art was full of this sort of lightness, in preference to the earlier heavier *Baroque*. Rococo emphasised surface decoration and used light pastel colours, e.g. pink, pale green, light blue, but eventually gave way to the stern moralising tone of *Neo-classicism*.

- **Who:** Boucher, Fragonard, Watteau.
- **When:** 1730–70/80.
- **Links:** to appreciate the decorativeness and lightness of Rococo, try comparing it to *realism*, especially the Rococo notion of the Fête Galante, the aristocratic open-air parties of the eighteenth century, with Manet's 'Dejeuner sur l'Herbe', 1863, Musée d'Orsay, Paris.
- **Formal elements:** all, especially pattern.

Romanticism: not so much a style as an approach. The key elements are individual experience and the importance of imagination; it is therefore often seen as the opposite of *classicism*. Romanticism started in Germany, expressing 'the voice from within' the artist, and was initially based largely on atmospheric landscape and the painting of ruins, which represent the infinite passing of time and the inability of man to understand it — see, for example, Caspar David Friedrich's 'The Wanderer above the Mists', 1817–18, Kunsthalle, Hamburg, in which a single, lonely figure stands on the top of a mountain staring down into a misty valley.

When Romanticism spread to France, it became more involved with public statements. One of the most powerful images is Eugene Delacroix's 'Liberty leading the People', 1830, Musée du Louvre, Paris, which shows an actual incident — the Parisian riots that led to the Revolution. Unlike earlier *Neoclassical* paintings of the same theme, e.g. David's 'Oath of the Horatii', Musée du Louvre, 1784, Paris, which works by classical reference, Delacroix's painting represents liberty as an *allegorical* but entirely believable figure, surrounded by workers in contemporary and suitably dirty clothing; the switch is from the representation of heroism to that of suffering.

Romantic art united reality with symbolic *idealism*. This depended on careful observation of nature and bright, vigorous *colour*. Delacroix's bright palette and his refusal to use black to create *tone* was particularly important for the later *Impressionists and Post-Impressionists*: Cézanne, for example, started as a Delacroix copyist.

■ *When:* late eighteenth to nineteenth century.

■ *Who:* Eugene Delacroix, Caspar David Friedrich, Theodore Gericault; in England: J. M. W. Turner, John Constable, William Blake.

■ *Links:* allegory, composition, colour, landscape, Neo-classicism, picturesque, Symbolism. Compare the composition of Gericault's 'Raft of the Medusa', 1819, Musée du Louvre, Paris, where a huge tilted raft juts into the pictorial space in a new formal arrangement, with Eugene Delacroix's 'Death of Sardanapulus', 1828, Musée du Louvre, which also features a vast rectangular form, in this case a bed, and more suffering. Note the frieze-like composition of Neo-classicism, e.g. the painting by David above, or the frantic claustrophobia of the *Expressionists*, e.g. Max Beckmann's 'The Night', 1918, Kunstsammlung Nordrhein-Westfalen, Dusseldorf, an extraordinary and confused scene of torture and murder. How does each artist compose the pictorial space? Why and what was each work made for? How does that function affect the composition? Bearing all this in mind, what will be the principles that guide your own composition?

The Romantic movement in painting and literature was responsible for the great interest in landscape, especially ruins and lonely, wild areas that had previously been ignored. Romanticism was not limited to the visual arts, and literature featured prominently — for example, the Lakeland poets, William Wordsworth and Samuel Taylor Coleridge, e.g. Wordsworth's 'Lines composed a few miles above Tintern Abbey', 1798. As a result of this sort of writing many artists visited areas like the Lakes to try to reproduce in paint what they had read about in words. The emotions created by a sense of place are central to Romanticism — is there any writing that would inspire you in the same way? It could be about a different type of landscape — the urban jungle, the suburban desert, the industrial wasteland.

Sacra Conversazione: paintings, often from Venice, showing the Virgin Mary and baby Jesus surrounded by saints, as though they were in conversation. In a *Sacra Conversazione* all the figures exist in the same pictorial space, e.g. San Giobbe Altarpiece, Giovanni Bellini, San Giobbe, Venice, before 1478. Earlier treatments of the same subject removed the saints to the wings of a *triptych* or the many panels of a *polyptych*.

■ *When:* from early fifteenth century Italy.

■ *Links: Renaissance, YBAs* (Damien Hirst's 'Mother and Child Divided').

Salon/Salon painting: exhibitions of the work of members of the French Royal Academy of Painting and Sculpture were held in the Salon d'Apollon in the Louvre. By the nineteenth century, the Salon had become the only annual public exhibition in Paris — unless your work had been shown at the Salon, it was impossible to sell. The Royal Academy in London operated in a similar manner. Work was only shown if it was accepted by an often elderly jury of artists, who did not encourage change or innovation. 'Salon painting' is the derogatory term for the academic and restrictive style (see *ideal*) that the Salon jury promoted. In 1863 the work of so many artists was rejected that the emperor ordered a Salon des Refusés to show their art. Among them were many of the artists we now think of as central to the history of art, e.g. Edouard Manet, Camille Pissarro, Paul Cézanne. After this, artists began to organise their own exhibitions and had much greater freedom to make what they wanted, so in many ways 1863 is the start of *Modernism*.

■ *When:* established in 1667, but most important in the nineteenth century.

■ *Links: Impressionism, Modernism, realism.*

saturation: also known as the purity or intensity of a *hue* (or *colour)*. Essentially, the saturation of a colour will lie somewhere between pure white at one end of an imaginary line through to the full intensity of the pure hue at the other end. True white, in the *additive* system of colour mixing, is made up from an equal mixture of the *primary colours*.

■ *Links:* colour, divisionism, primary colours.
■ *Formal elements:* colour.

screen printing/silk-screen printing: a type of stencil printing in which ink is forced through a screen, possibly silk, usually fine nylon mesh, stretched over a frame. Those areas of the screen that are blocked, either with a paper stencil, or painted out with a suitable medium or a photographically developed stencil, do not print, so will either read the white of the paper or whatever colour has been printed first. Screen printing is relatively cheap — these days *acrylic* paints and added printing media are used, which are forced through the mesh with a long rubber blade called a squeegee. The colour is applied in large, flat blocks and there is no form of blending or modulation.
■ *When:* first used as an artist's medium in America in the 1930s, but it became particularly prominent during Pop art in the 1960s.
■ *Who:* in the USA: Robert Rauschenberg and Andy Warhol; in the UK: Richard Hamilton.
■ *Links:* although Warhol's photo silk-screen prints are probably more familiar, e.g. 'Marilyn Diptych', 1962, Tate Modern, London, Robert Rauschenberg's silk-screen paintings might be more useful, e.g. 'Skyway', 1964, Dallas Museum of Art, USA. This is a work that uses oil paint and print in a *collage* of images that appear randomly selected, but in fact are carefully chosen, combining *gestural painting*, printed images and roughly applied colour. In the average art department it is difficult to find the space, time and equipment to work cleanly; this approach might solve that problem.
■ *Formal elements:* colour, pattern.

sculpture: the creation of form in three dimensions. Until 1912, this meant the two basic disciplines of *carving* and *modelling*, each having its own characteristics.

Carving is a reductive process: it removes material and shows a tendency for mass, solidity and weight, possibly a lack of intricate detail, and often the surface quality of the carved material reflects both the process that made it and the inherent qualities of the material itself. The weight of carved sculpture also makes it more difficult to develop open forms.

Modelling is an additive process, as it builds up form from nothing, e.g. adding clay onto clay to make a basis for a cast in bronze or plaster — a cast sculpture. This leads to different characteristics; because the original can be modelled, it allows for greater freedom and experimentation. After all, in carving you might carve off a piece but you cannot carve it back on again, whereas more modelling medium can always be added or removed. Modelling can create extended open forms, with intricate compositions, if the tensile strength of materials, e.g. bronze, allows. Modelling and subsequent casting allow a variety of surface textures, detail and qualities of cast material, e.g. *patina*.

In 1912, a new method of sculpture was added — *assemblage* — when Picasso made 'Guitar', Museum of Modern Art, New York, first out of cardboard and then from sheet metal. For the first time in the history of sculpture, an artist had assembled a work from open planes, rather than the solid mass of traditional weight. Not only that, 'Guitar' was put together from non-art materials in the same process as a Cubist *collage*.

Contemporary sculpture no longer uses the distinctions between the various disciplines, although Rachel Whiteread's 'House', made in 1993, and destroyed by the local Liberal council in 1994, was probably the largest cast work ever — a cast of the outside of a London terraced house (see *YBAs*). However, the majority of contemporary sculpture owes more to installation than carving or modelling, e.g. Tracey Emin's 'Bed', a presentation of the artist's bed in all its seedy glory, a work that has more to do with still life and self-portraiture than with the self-conscious creation of three-dimensional form.

■ *Links:* *Classical/classicism, Renaissance*. Picasso's 'Guitar' leads to Constructivist sculpture, e.g. Vladimir Tatlin's 'Proposed Model for the Monument to the Third International', 1919, Moderna Museet, Stockholm, to the abstract sculpture of Anthony Caro, e.g. 'Early One Morning', 1962, Tate Britain, London — one of the first truly abstract sculptures.

Most sculptors draw and it can be very useful to look at drawings whose main aim is to analyse form, e.g. Henry Moore's 'Women Winding Wool', 1949, Museum of Modern Art, New York. Some artists also use three-dimensional constructions to help create two-dimensional painted space, e.g. the Cornish artist, Peter Lanyon's construction, 'Coast Soaring', 1958, Private Collection, has a curved line of pipe next to a curved board. The same shape turns up in the later painting 'Lost Mine', 1959, Tate Gallery, St Ives. Lanyon also used precariously assembled planes of painted glass to examine ideas from every angle, e.g. 'Construction for St Just', 1952, Private Collection, which led to the painting 'St Just', 1953, Private Collection. These are processes that could help in the development of ideas, so do remember to keep, or at least document, all this research in your *work journal*.

scumble: a painting technique where one lighter opaque *colour* is rubbed or dragged over another darker colour, so that both layers are still visible — a method possible with both *oil* and *acrylic*.

■ *Links:* Rembrandt's 'A Woman Bathing in a Stream', 1655, National Gallery, London, shows how scumbling can be used to describe the different qualities and textures of cloth. Turner, who admired Rembrandt's techniques a great deal, uses scumbling for the altogether grander *landscape* effects in his 'Rain,

Steam and Speed', 1844, National Gallery, London, which shows a train on the new Great Western Railway powering across a bridge over the Thames, surrounded by light in a manner similar to the later *Impressionists*, e.g. 'Gare S. Lazare', 1877, Claude Monet, Musée d'Orsay, Paris.

Scumbling is a straightforward technique and, as you can see from the examples above, particularly suited for the visual research of *organic* subjects. Acrylic paint suits this technique well, because the underpainted layer needs to be fully dry before the top layer is put on, either with a palette knife, a dry brush or a bunched-up rag. You can of course build up as many layers as you like.

■ *Formal elements:* colour, texture.

secondary colours: the three colours that are made by mixing the *primary colours*: yellow and blue to make green, red and yellow to make orange, and red and blue to make purple.

■ *Links: colour, divisionism.*
■ *Formal elements:* colour.

sfumato: a style developed by Leonardo da Vinci, with soft transitions, in which outlines and colours are made hazy. The word comes from the Italian for smoky (see *aerial perspective* for greater detail).

shock: an important element in the work of *Modernist* artists and beyond, usually traced back to *Dada* and Marcel Duchamp (see *ready-made*) but increasingly difficult to achieve in a sated society, although the Chapman brothers' unpleasant phallic-nosed mannequins did well. It is noticeable that they trace their own work back to Goya, whose later work, especially the 'Disasters of War', 1810–20, was the inspiration for the brothers' 'Great Deeds against the Dead', 1994, a three-dimensional remake of the original Goya etching.

■ *Links: Dada.* Andy Warhol's 'Disaster Series' screen prints from the 1960s. Shock is difficult to use in an examined setting.

simultaneous contrast: a form of complementary contrast in which the eye makes the complementary contrast to another colour, so a red surface will be perceived, or seen with closed eyes, as green, and so on.

■ *Links:* used by *Impressionism.* As the contemporary scientist, Alfred de Lostalot, wrote: 'the clarity of the yellow rays [of the sun] stimulate the sensory mechanism of the painter, dazzling it, at the same time inducing in him the well-known physiological phenomenon known as the evoking of complementary colour: he sees violet. Those who love this colour will be gratified. M. Monet performs an exquisite symphony in violet for them'. See *Op art.*

site-specific: art made for a particular place and time, often some form of *installation.*

S

size: gelatine or purified glue which is painted onto a *canvas* or wooden panel to make it waterproof by filling up the pores. Canvas can be prepared by painting with cold-water glue size (or, as in the days of the artists' studios, size made from rabbit skin), which does not affect the colour of the canvas. The surface is then primed with a suitable white or mid-coloured *ground*, or left its natural colour and worked on without priming. Cold-water size (used to proof a wall before hanging wallpaper) is perfectly adequate and easily available from hardware stores or builders' merchants. Dilute with water according to the instructions on the packet. One coat will give a semi-porous surface to take a priming coat, two coats will make it more waterproof and ready to paint straight onto once it has dried — remember that wetting a canvas will tighten it up. These layers can be varied according to the medium you use: dilute *oil paint* will soak into a sized canvas far more than dilute *acrylic*, for example. Rabbit skin or hide glue is still available from artists' suppliers, but very expensive. It will need to be heated up in a special glue boiler, is smelly, and will offend vegetarians and those who love rabbits. Its preparation will also contravene any health and safety regulations you can think of.

Size *colour* is a method of painting in which powdered pigment is mixed into hot glue size to make a painting medium for large areas. It is quick to use, but fragile, and in these days of cheap emulsion paint, if size colour is used at all, it is for scene painting.

■ *Links: canvas, ground.*

Socialist Realism: the official art of the USSR and of other Communist countries, which used an *idealised*, populist, *naturalistic* style to make huge images that borrowed from history painting and *Neo-classicism* to show scenes of the good life under Socialism.

■ *When:* 1932 to the 1950s.

■ *Links: history painting, Nazi art.* Do not confuse Socialist Realism with Social Realism, which describes political art produced by left-wing artists during the 1920s and 1930s, e.g. the Mexican *frescoes* of Diego Rivera and Jose Orozco.

still life: one of the *Genres* of art. A precise definition is not easy but the French term for still life, 'nature morte', describes it best; essentially a study of things that do not move. A still life shows inanimate objects such as fruit, flowers, dead animals or everyday objects. It was the insignificance of the objects portrayed that placed still lives so low in the hierarchy of Genres. A still life can be part of a larger painting or, more properly, a subject in its own right, and there are many variations on the basic type: flower painting, fruit and vegetables, **Vanitas**, symbolic or *allegorical* paintings, game (dead animals and birds), or a general collection of the everyday and ordinary clutter in the artist's studio — often items that look as if they will become the artist's lunch.

■ *When:* still life as a subject can be found in ancient Roman wall paintings, e.g. Pompeii, and continues through to the present day in one form or another; for example the American artist, Jeff Koons, took a series of different types of ordinary domestic objects such as the vacuum cleaner, and presented them in perspex cases, with their own internal lighting — see 'New Hoover Quadraflex', 'New Hoover Convertible', 'New Hoover Dimension 900', and 'New Hoover Dimension 1000 Doubledecker', 1981–86, Deitch Projects, New York. To an extent these are a reworking of Duchamp's *ready-mades*, but it is the fact that Koons described them as beautiful objects in their own right, and that the Hoovers are brand new, which relates them more closely to everyday life. They are examples of the everyday objects of desire that were often the subject of still life studies in the past. The high points of still life painting are probably the Netherlands in the seventeenth century and early *Modernist* artists, especially *Cubism*.

■ *Who:* most artists paint still life, either as a personal exercise or as an object to sell, but Chardin, e.g. 'Still Life with Ray Fish', 1728, Musée du Louvre, Paris, and Paul Cézanne, e.g. 'Still life with Plaster Cupid', 1895, Courtauld Gallery, London, both concentrated on the Genre.

■ *Links: allegory, Genre,* **trompe l'oeil, Vanitas.** Flower paintings are not as straightforward as they look; they often have symbolic meanings. There is a language of flowers and specific flowers have particular associations: white lilies were used for the Annunciation, when the angel Gabriel announces to Mary she will bear Christ, honeysuckle was a symbol of the Holy Spirit, strawberry blossom represented the flowers of paradise and the food of children who had died prematurely. These are all associations that are worth pursuing — many Dutch flower paintings are complex arguments for a particular form of Christianity. There is something appealing about making a still life that appears calm, but in fact contains a serious argument. What should a contemporary still life contain?

stipple: a painting technique using small dots or a dabbing motion. Keeping a blunt-ended, bristle brush at right angles to the work, it gives a textured surface.
■ *Links: brush, Impressionism.*

subtractive mixing: when one *primary colour* (red, yellow or blue) is mixed with another, the result is called a *secondary colour* (green, violet or orange). Each new pigment that is added darkens the mixture, so that in theory after many mixes the result will be black. This process is known as subtractive mixing because the colour added takes away or absorbs more waves from white light (ordinary daylight) than the initial colour did. The effect of mixing many colours is to make the final colour duller, or muddy looking. There are various methods of keeping the brightness of colours. For instance, viridian is a bright

S

emerald green (also known as hydrated chromium hydroxide), of a pure clear tone — a single pigment. Try comparing it with a mixture of yellow and blue; two pigments mixed together have the inevitable subtractive result. The *Neo-Impressionist* artists, Seurat and Signac, used optical mixing (see *divisionism*), blending colours in the eye, not on the palette; try the same system yourself.

■ *Links:* additive mixing, cloisonnisme, colour, complementary colours, divisionism, hue, saturation, secondary colours, simultaneous contrast.

■ *Formal elements:* tone, colour.

Suprematism: Russian *abstract* art developed by Kasimir Malevich. His Suprematist paintings were probably the first purely abstract paintings in the Western tradition, e.g. 'Suprematist Square', 1914–15, Tretyakov, Moscow. As the title suggests, this a pure black square but painted onto a slightly larger square white canvas so that the border shows. It is not a painting of objects; the shape of the square does not come from nature or *organic* forms but comes from standard geometric shapes. Later in 1918 he painted pure white squares. Suprematist paintings were certainly the first since the *Renaissance* to remove the *illusion* of modelled form and pictorial depth, so that the responses come solely from purely geometrical, abstract forms. Suprematism, like the equally utopian *De Stijl* in Holland, tried to represent the higher order of the non-objective world or the fourth dimension, the abstract spiritual energy that connects and moves the concrete world — 'the supremacy of pure feeling'. You can see an attempt to analyse this in Malevich's 'Suprematism: Painterly Realism of a Football Player (Colour Masses of the Fourth Dimension)', 1915, Stedelijk Museum, Amsterdam. This is an entirely abstract painting with none of the usual references to football the viewer might expect from such a title.

■ *When:* 1915–18.

■ *Who:* Kasimir Malevich, El Lissitsky, Laszlo Moholy-Nagy.

■ *Links:* abstract, Bauhaus, Constructivism, De Stijl, Futurism. Malevich said that 'the square is not a subconscious form. It is the creation of intuitive reason. The face of the new art. The square is the living, royal, infant. It is the first step of pure creation in art'. Can a single shape hold this sort of weight? If so, what shapes should you work with now?

Surrealism: a movement of writers, artists and filmmakers based around the writer André Breton in Paris, who formally founded the movement in 1924. The key Surrealist intention was to discover and release the creative power of the imagination and the subconscious, to capture the irrational and uncontrollable that we normally only get to through dreams.

The term was first used by the writer Guillaume Apollinaire in Paris in 1917; he said that 'the artistic truth resulting from a combination of elements was a truth beyond realism...a kind of sur-realism'. 'Surrealism is not a style. It is the cry of a mind turning back on itself' (Antonin Artaud). Surrealism was not an identifiable style, like, for instance, *Cubism* — Surrealists deliberately upset the conscious mind by using the unconscious; the unconscious mind was called 'the marvellous'. Surrealist art was an attempt to represent and analyse the process of thought using many different techniques, for instance *automatic writing*, *decalcomania*, *frottage* and a series of games. Remember the date and the place Surrealism started. Early Surrealists saw the madness of the world's first mechanised war, the First World War, as the result of political reason. They looked to the illogical, to 'the marvellous' as an alternative to the hopelessness created by man's conscious thought.

Later Surrealists (from about 1929) became more interested in dreams and trying to represent them. Their dream paintings are very minutely detailed and show unlikely objects in curious settings. Dali or Magritte are the obvious examples. Surrealists also used objects; the Surrealist object was often a real thing, e.g. a cup and saucer, that had been treated in some way (covered in fur) intended to open up the unconscious mind — Meret Oppenheim's 'Luncheon in Fur', 1936, Museum of Modern Art, New York. Surrealism and *Dada* were closely interlinked, as were the Surrealist object and the *ready-made*. Of the Surrealist films, the most famous was probably Luis Buñuel's and Salvador Dali's *Un Chien andalou* of 1929, which has a notorious scene in which a razor blade is drawn across a woman's eyeball superimposed on a cloudy sky. Surrealist images have been an endless reference point for art, film and, especially, advertising ever since: 'Bringing widely separate realities together and drawing a spark from their contact', wrote André Breton. 'As beautiful as the chance encounter of an umbrella and a sewing machine on a dissecting table' (Comte de Lautréamont, the nineteenth-century poet whom the Surrealists considered their predecessor).

■ *When:* 1924–45.
■ *Who:* Hans Arp, Salvador Dali, Max Ernst, René Magritte, Man Ray, André Masson, Joan Miró and many more.
■ *Links: Abstract Expressionism, Dada, ready-made, Symbolism.*
■ *Formal elements:* all.

Symbolism: a loosely organised artistic movement, both literary and visual, which investigated mystical, *allegorical* and spiritual subjects, rejecting the direct recording of optical reality that was the declared aim of *Impressionism*. Apart from this general anti-realism, there was no overall style. Symbolism emphasised the emotions art aroused in the viewer, but this led artists to investigate the formal qualities of paintings with care, moving away from their descriptive ability and finding out which arrangements created which effects. Artists realised that *colour* and *line* could express ideas in themselves and they tended to flatten their pictorial forms and stress their decorative qualities: 'It is well to remember that before being a battle horse, a nude woman or some anecdote, it is essentially a flat surface coloured with colours assembled in a certain order', Maurice Denis, 1890.

■ *When:* 1885–1910.

■ *Who:* Gauguin and Odilon Redon. Various artists went through a Symbolist period, e.g. Piet Mondrian's tree paintings that start as Symbolist metaphors (see *De Stijl*) but eventually become purely abstract. The paintings of Edvard Munch can fit into both Symbolism and *Expressionism*.

■ *Links:* allegory, primitivism, realism, Romanticism, Surrealism.

■ *Formal elements:* all.

Synthetic Cubism: see *Cubism*.

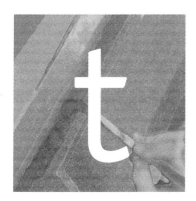

tempera: the usual medium for panel painting in the Middle Ages and the *Renaissance,* until the invention of oil paint. The binders of **tempera** paints (often egg yolk — apparently town chickens produced the most suitable pale yolks) are diluted in water, but are not water-soluble once dry. Egg **tempera** dried very quickly and so could only be painted in small areas at a time, *colours* were few and difficult to blend, and the range of effects depended on the slow building up of layers of semi-transparent paint on top of solid underpainting. For instance, to make flesh colour, tints had to be painted onto a green under-painting (**terre verte**). Often those top layers have faded, leaving some strangely green faces, e.g. Duccio di Buoninsegna's 'Annunciation', 1311, National Gallery, London, a small panel from a larger altarpiece, an early Renaissance work. The green underpainting is starting to show through in the faces.

■ *When:* thirteenth to fifteenth centuries, particularly important during the Early Italian Renaissance.

■ *Links:* oil paint, Renaissance.

theme/thematic: the majority of work made for examination at AS/A-level is thematic, that is to say, it is made in response to a concept, brief idea or starting point. Ideas are the starting point for most art and design and they are essential for the creative process. Remember that a theme is not a question as such — a question requires a specific answer whereas the thematic approach should stimulate your personal response and route to an outcome.

tonal colour/tonal values/tone: one of the *formal elements,* the building blocks of art, meaning the rendering of light. Most students are familiar with this as shading, usually done with a soft pencil. Tonal values are the gradual moving of tone from light to dark, which you can see on any solid object under light: the lightest areas (highlights), the darkest areas and the values in between (midtones). Tone is seen as separate from *local colour* (the different *colours* of that same object under light), so tonal colours are an attempt to represent the degrees of light falling on an object rather than its range of perceived colours.

Traditionally the way to see this play of light is to half-close your eyes. The logical approach would be to use the range from black to white, but in practice you will need to include a subtle range of other colours, usually yellow at the highlights and possibly blue for the darkest tones. Remember that you do not have to use black and white — any restricted palette will do, as long as the range and proportion of tonal values you paint or draw are the same as those of your subject.

■ *Links:* colour, divisionism, Impressionism.
■ *Formal elements:* tone, colour, form.

trecento: Italian term for the fourteenth century, i.e. 1300s.

Trinity: The three divine characters in the Christian religion: Father, Son and Holy Ghost, who combine together to form the one God.

triptych: three paintings hinged together to make a picture of three sections, particularly applied to winged altars with a larger central panel that shows Christ or perhaps the Virgin Mary. On the side panels, which can be folded over to protect the centre, are often paintings of the donors who paid for the work, as well as the relevant saints for the church that commissioned the work, e.g. Duccio's 'The Virgin and Child with Saint Dominic and Saint Aurea', 1310–20, National Gallery, London.

■ *When:* although known in antiquity, really a Christian function dating from twelfth-century Italy.
■ *Links:* diptych, Renaissance.

trompe l'oeil: see *illusion*.

Turner Prize: started in 1984, this is an annual prize of £20,000, organised by the Patrons of New Art, part of the Friends of the Tate Gallery, London. From a short list of four the prize is now awarded to 'a British artist under 50 for an outstanding exhibition or other presentation of their work in the 12 months preceding'. The Turner's aim is 'to promote public discussion of new developments in British art' and because it is sponsored by Channel 4 television, controversy and hype become part of the annual event. As a result of the criteria, the prize has been won by some of those British artists who use the media well, e.g. Gilbert and George in 1987, and many of the *YBAs* — Rachel Whiteread in 1993, when she was only 30, and Damien Hirst in 1995. As Howard Hodgkin, a member of the older generation of British artists who won in 1986, said: 'It's quite lonely making art of any sort, so the more attention young artists get the better they like it…most young artists want hype. They want people to know what they're doing, and they want people to see it. A bit of pressure and media attention seems a small price to pay.'

Artists now deal directly with the culture they have grown up in. The issues are morality, mortality, memory, perception and materialism, rather than pure mark-making.

■ *When:* annually since 1984.

■ *Links: Modernism, postmodernism, shock, YBAs.*

turning edge: a term for an element used in creating the *illusion* of three-dimensionality on a two-dimensional surface, in particular where an artist has used *tone* or *colour* to describe how an object appears to move away from the eye — the rim of a jug perhaps or the curve of an arm. The qualities used in creating the turning edge are often taken by examiners as a good clue to a candidate's overall craft skills.

vanishing lines: see *orthogonals*.

vanishing point: in the theory of *perspective*, the point at which parallel lines meet in infinity. For example, parallel railway lines appear to meet on the horizon at the vanishing point.

Vanitas*:** *allegorical* works that contained symbols of time passing, such as a skull, an hourglass, a bubble or a burned-down candle. It was an important branch of *still life* painting, particularly in seventeenth-century Holland. The name comes from the biblical phrase 'vanity of vanities; all is vanity', meaning that owning too many worldly possessions is pointless, if life is so short and the afterlife so long — see 'The Vanities of Human Life' by Harman Steenwyck, 1645, National Gallery, London, a painting with many of the ***Vanitas images: the skull a ***memento mori*** (souvenir or reminder of death); the musical instruments, many of which are symbols of lust and its outcome, pregnancy; the wisp of smoke and the open book representing the pointlessness of book learning in eternity. For a ***Vanitas*** painting to work, the objects have to be painted with great skill — the illusion of their actual presence needs to be as strong as possible. These paintings are also relatively small, and their domestic scale tells us that they were meant for the home, rather than to be hung in more public places. They were visual sermons to remind you to be good each day.

■ ***When:*** sixteenth century onwards, but in one sense all still life paintings of organic objects are investigations of the ***Vanitas*** theme; after all, everything must pass and whatever is painted will eventually rot away, as will the artist who painted it and the viewer looking at the art.

■ ***Links:*** *allegory, Genre, illusion, still life*. Both Cézanne ('Pyramid of Skulls', 1900, Private Collection) and Andy Warhol ('Skulls', 1976, Andy Warhol Foundation, New York) made images of skulls towards the end of their lives. Were these updating the ***Vanitas*** themes, or just premonitions of their own death?

What objects would a modern ***Vanitas*** painting contain? Think of not just luxury goods as images of wealth, but also objects that symbolise time passing quickly. Try also to be more inventive with your choice of ***memento mori*** — find something other than a skull.

verisimilitude: see *illusion*.

visual language: a common form of communication and expression using signs, symbols and everything that can be seen, in the same way that we use a fundamental system of words called language to communicate meaning. It is the job of the artist, craftsperson or designer to investigate and extend this language through making objects, and by looking at what others have done in the past and are doing now.

vitrine: a glass box for displaying works of art or curios, and the name given to the glass boxes containing Damien Hirst's preserved animals, e.g. 'The Physical Impossibility of Death in the Mind of Someone Living', 1991, Saatchi Collection, London, a 4-metre tiger shark suspended in a huge tank (vitrine) of formaldehyde.

wash: a very thin layer of diluted ink or *watercolour* paint, so thin as to be almost transparent, spread evenly over a large area, without showing the brushwork. A layer of washes can be built up to produce a solid body of colour in some parts of the work.

■ *Links: watercolour* is the obvious application of this technique — try the difference between applying washes of paint to wet and dry paper (note: you will need to stretch the paper absolutely flat to apply a uniform wash of colour; otherwise where the colour puddles, it will become darker).

Morris Louis, the American artist, used washes of *acrylic* paints on unprimed *canvas*, e.g. 'Gamma Delta', 1959–60, Whitney Museum, New York. His late paintings were very precise and deliberate patterns of poured paint, thicker than pure washes; nevertheless the texture of the canvas can still be seen through them.

■ *Formal elements:* tone, colour, texture.

watercolour: water-soluble pigments, which dry transparent, and so look particularly light and delicate.

■ *When:* used on white paper, there is therefore no white watercolour pigment — that role is taken by the white paper *ground*. This property means that in putting on the paint you are working from light to dark, rather than the other way around, which you are probably more familiar with. This type of painting, sometimes called **aquarelle**, is used mostly for small-scale work and so is very suitable for working outside, e.g. *landscapes*.

■ *Links:* there is a long tradition of English landscape watercolourists. The most prominent examples are probably J. M. W. Turner, Thomas Girtin, and the Norwich School, e.g. John Sell Cotman. Paul Cézanne's late watercolours are also well worth looking at. For example, his watercolours of Monte Sainte Victoire, 1900–06, Tate Modern, London, show him using the length of the sable *brush* to make shapes that indicate the distance between the subject he is looking at and the artist's eye. Look also at his late still life watercolours, modelling form through layers of colour, and particularly at the way he tries to describe the *turning edge* — for example, 'Apples, Bottles, Chair Back' 1902–06, Courtauld Gallery, London.

The watercolour technique depends on a series of *washes*. Try the difference between working 'wet into wet' when the underlying colour is not yet dry, and putting one onto another once it is dry. Which works best for the subject you are tackling? Why? Compare this to the methods of the artist you have been studying with a series of *annotated* images of their work and yours.

woodcut: like lino cut, this is a *relief* printing technique in which the area around the image is cut out, in this case from a flat piece of wood (the block). When the block is inked up and placed on a sheet of paper, only those raised parts left will print; that which has been cut away will not show, unlike ***intaglio*** techniques where the ink is kept in the grooves to make a print.

■ *Links:* ***intaglio***, *mono printing, relief.* Japanese woodcuts were especially sophisticated, using flat blocks of colour and compositional techniques that heavily influenced *Post-Impressionist* artists like van Gogh. Woodcut was important in the early years of the twentieth century for the *Expressionists*; Edvard Munch made many woodcut versions of his famous 'Scream' image. *Die Brücke* in particular used woodcut, e.g. Erich Heckel's coloured woodcut, 'Portrait of a Man', 1919, Staatsgalerie, Stuttgart, where the black outlines of the strongly-cut head and hands of the figure are printed onto thick *washes* of colour.

The importance of woodcut at this level is that you do not need a press to get a suitable print, only a stiffish ink (paint will run into the cut-away areas and smudge, so use specialist relief printing ink) and a strong hand. Ink is applied with a roller, the block is laid ink-side up and paper put on top of it. Rub the back of the paper with the back of a spoon, or the traditional tool, a burin, or just the back of your hand, working in a circular motion from the centre. Any material can make a block; a strong grain, e.g. pine, will make a very powerful image, although the softness of the wood makes a detailed image difficult. Try experimenting with other materials, for instance an old formica work surface which can be scratched and cut into to make an image, as can other already textured surfaces, e.g. chipboard, fibreboard. You do not need specialist cutting tools, although good woodcutting chisels or even lino cutters help a great deal. Most surfaces can be cut with a Stanley knife: make a stroke with the blade of the knife at right angles to the block, make a second stroke with the blade at an angle to the first so that you have cut away a v-shaped groove, and vary the angle of the second cut to change the effect. But take care — always cut away from you, never towards your hand, and do not put the blade under such pressure that it might break.

■ *Formal elements:* line, pattern, texture.

Essential Word Dictionary

work journal: more than just a sketchbook, the work journal is a process, a way of working, of showing the development of your ideas, including art studies, visual research, evaluations, planning and the development of your art. Think carefully about the way you present your work journals: do they reflect the art and design that you make and have studied? If, for instance, your work is clean and crisp and you have perhaps studied someone like Hockney, or the abstract work of *De Stijl*, is your work journal laid out with bold sharp-edged areas of primary colour or large white spaces, clean text, handwritten as if it was Hockneyesque? You should use a suitable font from among the thousands of fonts available on computers for word processing; there is a De Stijl font, for example. Can anyone looking at the journals see you developing ways of displaying the journals themselves? Review is the key word here. Go back through the work for each unit and comment on it yourself, dating those comments. By writing them in a new way you can show what you have learnt since you started — you are displaying progression.

YBAs: also known as Brit art, the YBAs was the name given to art made by a generation of British artists from the late twentieth century, most of whom were students at Goldsmiths Art College, London, in the late 1980s. Their work came to major international prominence when it was bought by the advertising millionaire and art collector, Charles Saatchi, and shown in the 'Sensation' exhibition at the Royal Academy London, 1997. The excitement generated by their large, usually, though not predominantly, three-dimensional work, briefly made London the capital of *avant-garde* art. There is no particular Brit art style, although Damien Hirst is often quoted as the unofficial group leader. His 'Mother and Child Divided' from 1993, Saatchi Collection, London, is a good example. This work shows a cow and her calf suspended in formalde-hyde. Each animal has been cut in half and is separated not only from its relative, but also from itself and separated from the surrounding world by the glass case (*vitrine*) in which they are displayed/preserved. The melancholy feeling of such a work and its analysis of death, alienation and previous art is characteristic of many YBA works, although the insistence on death is peculiar to Damien Hirst. 'Mother and Child Divided' was first shown in Venice, home to important paintings and mosaics about the Virgin Mary. What linked the YBA artists was youth, a common sponsor (Charles Saatchi), a general use of the basic aims of *Conceptual art*, and a familiarity in their dealings with the media; this was the first artistic generation of the television age.

■ *Who:* the most famous names are probably Damien Hirst and Tracey Emin; others include Jake and Dinos Chapman, Gary Hume and Chris Ofili. Rachel Whiteread is often included, although she is older than most of the rest of the YBAs and her work has more in common with the *Minimalist/Conceptualist* era, e.g. 'House', 1993, destroyed 1994 — the cast of the entire outside of an east London terraced house.

■ *Links: avant-garde, shock*. The artists with the greatest influence on this generation were Gilbert and George, who became living sculptures in the 1960s. Their huge photo pieces, e.g. 'Death Hope Life Fear', 1984, Tate Modern,

London, deal with contemporary themes, are often shocking and are certainly designed to upset middle-class audiences. They took the collage approach, e.g. the influence of Kurt Schwitters (see *Dada*).

Tracey Emin's autobiographical approach is worth considering, although her rawness is not always applicable. The diary method of combining visual research with personal development has a long and justifiable history. The statement designed solely to *shock* can be self-indulgent, but with a developing personal visual language and analysis of the past, it can have a future.

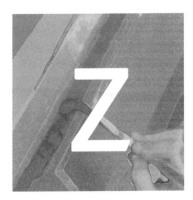

Zeitgeist: a German word meaning spirit of the age. All art, one way or another, will reflect the period in which it is made, but most *avant-garde* art takes analysing, if not creating, the feeling of the times as one of its major subjects. The **Zeitgeist**, then, is an important part of many *Modernist* art works. This might be straightforward, as in Edouard Manet's 'Music in the Tuileries Gardens', 1860–62, National Gallery, London, which shows the fashionable upper classes of Paris stepping out into the newly-made outdoor areas of the rebuilt city, a crowd dotted with Manet's friends and those thinkers he considered important, e.g. the critic Baudelaire (see *realism*). Or it might be part of the manner of painting, e.g. the *Expressionist* painter Ernst Ludwig Kirchner's aggressive, primitive images of prostitutes and businessmen on the streets of Berlin, like his *woodcut* 'Women at Potsdamer Platz', 1914. Or it might be in the style of presentation of an installation, e.g. Damien Hirst's 'Pharmacy', 1992, Tate Modern, London — a complete chemist's shop installed in an art gallery, making the viewer think of death and the faith we have in science to keep us alive, displayed in a semi-*Minimalist* setting.

Bibliography

Critical and contextual studies (art studies)

Berger, J. (1987) *Ways of Seeing*, Pelican.

Blazwick, I. and Wilson, S. (2000) *Tate Modern, the Handbook*, Tate Publishing. Very useful run-down on most art movements since Impressionism, with excellent pictures. The book to read before any visit to Tate Modern.

Butler, A., Cleave, C.V. and Stirling, S. (eds) (1999) *The Art Book*, Phaidon. The small version of a larger book, a good pocket-size collection of images.

Chilvers, I. and Osbourne, H. (eds) (1997) *The Oxford Dictionary of Art*, Oxford University Press. Your *Essential Word Dictionary* does not contain biographies, and you might need greater detail. Of the many art dictionaries around, the Oxford dictionary is probably one of the best, certainly on the modern movement.

Cummin, R. (1997) *Annotated Guide to Art*, Dorling Kindersley. There are many versions of this way of approaching art, and *annotation* is a key skill in examined art nowadays. Dorling Kindersley also publishes small books on individual artists that can be equally useful, but remember your aim is analysis, not biography.

Fineberg, J. (2000) *Art Since 1940, Strategies of Being* (2nd edn), Laurence King. Very useful for post-Second World War art movements, especially the American ones.

Gombrich, E. H. (1999) *The Story of Art*, Phaidon. The standard progressive history of art, i.e. this movement led to this movement which led to that one. Every art teacher will have read this book, but it is still quite useful. Good pictures as well, though Gombrich finds any art after Impressionism a little hard to get excited about.

Gordon, D. (1988) *The National Gallery, London*, National Gallery Publications. The current guide to the National Gallery can be very helpful when working on contextual studies. These sort of guides are also a great help when planning a trip to a gallery, in order to find out exactly which works to see.

Hugh, H. and Fleming, J. (1999) *A World History of Art*, Laurence King. The standard art history text, it is expensive but useful to consult if you can find a library with a reference copy. The text is in short sections covering every art movement since the Neolithic, although some parts are vague.

Hughes, R. (1991) *The Shock of the New*, London. An excellent book on the history of Modernism, based on a television series made in the 1980s, so very readable.

Movements in Modern Art series, Tate Publishing. These are on various themes from realism to postmodernism and beyond, with many more titles to come in the future. Although they tend to be academic and sometimes quite difficult to read, with concentration they are all well worth the effort, and the pictures of key works are always very good.

Rainer Hagen, R. and R-M. (2000) *What Great Paintings Say*, Taschen. Taschen Publishing produces an enormous number of reasonably priced books on every type of art. Its smaller series of books on individual artists are often very good, but because they are cheap they fall apart quickly.

Sturgis, E. A. (2000) *Understanding Paintings*, Mitchell Beazley.

Methods and materials

Cole, A. (1992) *Perspective*, Dorling Kindersley in association with the National Gallery. As you would expect from Dorling Kindersley books, this is properly illustrated to explain the mysteries of perspective. It shows well-known paintings from the National Gallery and, usefully, it has sections on later Modernist paintings and their use of space, from Cubism to Pop art. There are also Dorling Kindersley books on the techniques of painting and drawing, as well as the properties of colour.

Mayer, R. (1991) *The Artist's Handbook of Materials and Techniques*, Faber and Faber. This standard guide to all artists' materials is an enormous book and expensive, so mainly useful as a reference book. It contains more or less everything you need to know, especially about materials for two-dimensional surfaces. If you want to know how to make traditional egg *tempera* (separate yolk from white, grind pigment into paste and mix directly into the yolk), the colour of gamboge (yellow) or where the hair in camel hair brushes comes from (squirrels' tails), then this is the book for you.

Smith, R. (1991) *The Artist's Handbook*, Dorling Kindersley. Only about painting, drawing and printmaking, but an easier book to approach than the Mayer above. Much better on basic techniques, although less authoritative on materials, it does have colour illustrations, which are useful for the sections on colour.

Websites

These change constantly. Due to copyright, most sites, especially those featuring art made after about 1960, will not let you download or print images. There are two important things to remember about using the internet for art:

- there is more to an art study, a major Contextual Study unit or a piece of analytical work than a cut and pasted image (see *annotation*)
- monitor how long you are spending looking for that vital image or piece of information. It is easy to waste valuable hours searching for something that is in the book on the shelf beside you. As a general rule, look in the book first — it is quicker

Museums and galleries

Every major museum has its own website, some of which are excellent, featuring virtual walkthroughs of their rooms, as well as information and access to images. Most substantial galleries display some sort of information as well. This is by no means an exhaustive list.

Art Institute of Chicago
http://www.artic.edu

The Getty Museum, Los Angeles
http://www.getty.edu

Musée du Louvre, Paris
http://www.louvre.fr

Metropolitan Museum of Art, New York
http://www.metmuseum.org

Museum of Modern Art, New York
http://www.moma.org

National Gallery, London
http://www.nationalgallery.org.uk

National Portrait Gallery, London
http://www.npt.org.uk

The Rijksmuseum, Amsterdam
http://www.rijksmuseum.nl

Royal Academy, London
http://www.royalacademy.org.uk

Tate Galleries, London
http://www.tate.org

24 Hour Museum
http://www.24hourmuseum.org.uk

Useful sites

There are various artist index sites, the most useful of which are:
http://www.oir.ucf.edu/wm/paint/auth/
http://www.artcyclopedia.com

See also:
http://www.art.net.com
http://www.artupdate.com
http://www.artchive.com
http://www.dare.online.org
http://www.educationunlimited.so.uk/netclass/schools/art
http://www.netart-netart.com
http://wwar.com

There are thousands of art history sites, mostly linked to American universities. Many are too text based and difficult to understand, but some are useful:

http://www.Anu.edu.au/index
http://www.harbrace.com/art/gardner
http://www.umich.edu/~umma/